Go Pack Go –

Tony Walter
July 2022

Ice Bowl

The Game That Will Never Die

Tony Walter

M&B Global Solutions Inc.
Green Bay, Wisconsin (USA)

Ice Bowl
The Game That Will Never Die

Front cover photo: Green Bay Packers fans tear down the goalposts in the aftermath of their team's victory over the Dallas Cowboys in the 1967 NFL Championship Game, commonly known as the Ice Bowl. (*Photo courtesy of Paul Vidani*)

Back cover photo: Packers quarterback Bart Starr (15) sneaks across the goal line for the winning touchdown behind a clearing block by guard Jerry Kramer (64). (*Photo courtesy of the Green Bay Press-Gazette*)

ISBN: 978-1-942731-43-6

Published by M&B Global Solutions Inc.
Green Bay, Wisconsin (USA)

Dedication

She gets credit for being one of the people who sat at Lambeau Field for the Ice Bowl. She gets credit for suggesting I write a book about the stories surrounding the Ice Bowl.

And she gets credit for tolerating the stacks of notebooks in the den, the absences when I traveled back to Green Bay to do research (although I always brought some Seroogy's caramels back with me), and the fifty-plus years listening to me talk about the Packers.

So this book is for you, Jenny.

Contents

Foreword

By Chuck Mercein

Green Bay Packers Running Back in the Ice Bowl

The Ice Bowl has meant so much to me personally that it cannot be overstating it to say this game was the defining moment in my football career.

I'd like to thank Tony Walter for inviting me to write this foreword to his new book on the Ice Bowl. Even though so much time has passed since that iconic battle, the Ice Bowl still resonates with me as though it was played only months, weeks, or days ago. But back in the day when we actually did play the game in the worst possible conditions ever, with temperatures as low as

-16 degrees and with wind chill factors as low as -56 degrees, no one could imagine that the Ice Bowl was to become arguably the most famous game in NFL history.

What remained for me to find out, though, was how impactful that final drive was going to be for me not just in my legacy as a Green Bay Packer, but even more to my reputation throughout my life.

With a little more than four minutes to go in the game and with Green Bay trailing 17-14, we started our final drive 68 yards away from paydirt. Donny Anderson ran for three yards on our first play, and I ran a dive off right tackle for seven yards and our first big first down of the drive. I remember it well as we were on the short side of the field right alongside the Packers' bench. I can still vividly recall Coach Lombardi yelling, "That a way, Chuck!"

What a feeling!

After Anderson caught a couple swing passes out of the backfield for another first down, I did something I'd never done before. I told Bart Starr on the way back into the huddle that I was open in the left flat if he needed me. Sure enough, he hit me on a swing pass out of the backfield on the very next play, which resulted in a big 19-yard gain down to the 11-yard line before I dove out of bounds, saving us our last timeout. Cowboys coach Tom Landry, I was told later, said that was the play that broke the Cowboys' back.

It was now my turn again as Starr called what he later described as the best call he ever made in his long career. It was the "54 Give" play on which I barreled up the middle for another eight yards down to the 3-yard line. I later learned that I had personally accounted for half the yards, 34 of 68, in that final great drive.

Chuck Mercein (No. 30 in the center of the pile) holds his arms up to show the referees that he was not aiding Bart Starr on his quarterback sneak to win the Ice Bowl, which would have been a penalty. (Photo courtesy of the Green Bay Press-Gazette)

We then tried Anderson on two dives between guard and tackle, which gained us only a couple of yards. Bart called our final timeout as he trudged to the sideline to discuss with Coach Lombardi what our last ditch chance play would be, since we had no more timeouts and there were only 16 seconds left on the clock.

I had no doubt that the call also would be to me with it being "31 Wedge," a simple dive between center Ken Bowman and guard Jerry Kramer. The "wedge" blocking scheme on the play entailed a double team, with Kramer driving low into defensive tackle Jethro Pugh.

Starr easily snuck the ball over himself for the final yard for the TD. The only thing about the play, however, was that Bart never told us in the huddle that he was going to keep the ball himself rather than risk any kind of a miscue if he handed off the ball to me as the play was designed to do.

There's a story behind the iconic picture showing No. 30 (me) looming over Starr's outstretched body over the goal line with my hands held up as if I'm signaling a TD. I was actually not doing any such thing, but rather trying to show the referees that I was not in any way aiding and abetting Bart's plunge, which would have been a penalty at that time.

All's well that ends well, though, and the important thing was, of course, that the play was a success and we won the game.

Little did I know at the time that, as the late Steve Sabol of NFL Films later told me, the Ice Bowl would become the most rebroadcast football game in NFL history. I never realized that I'd still be receiving fan mail to this very day every week asking me for autographs, including on my old football cards and on that cover of *Sports Illustrated* I was on the week after the game.

I am still surprised, and always will be humbled, by such recognition, whether it be from the average fan or from the more famous, such as one of my favorite actors and comedians, Bill Murray. I recently was introduced to him at my golf club, Winged Foot, in Mamaroneck, New York. His first words to me were, "Chuck Mercein, the Ice Bowl. Good to meet you."

My own kids love to tease me about the Ice Bowl, often calling it, "The game that will never die!"

And actually, they're right.

Chuck Mercein displays the Sports Illustrated cover on which he appeared on January 8, 1968. The issue came out after the NFL and AFL championship games, and hyped Super Bowl II, which the Packers would win on January 14, 1968, over the Oakland Raiders. (Photo courtesy of Chuck Mercein)

"What They Saw Was a Drama"

(Excerpt from Bob Woessner's article in the Green Bay Press-Gazette, *Tuesday, January 2, 1968.)*

There was ... glory in the stands where a horde of frozen fanatics watched the proceedings in weather that would have sent the Abominable Snowman to winter quarters. It was a day better suited for the defense of Stalingrad or for sniping at Napoleon as he crept home across the plain.

It was a day that the capacity crowd will long remember – as people today recall how they got through the Depression of the 1930s or where they were when World War II ended.

There is also a suspicion that a generation from now the crowd that shivered and wheezed its way through this one will number in the hundreds of thousands.

Bob Woessner

The man who lives here knows why, and how, they do it. This Packer crowd was no mere bunch of thrill seekers or sports fans. They showed, just by being there and enduring what they did, what this team is all about. Those stands had to be filled Sunday – despite the conditions – because this was Green Bay and the Packers were playing for the biggest championship in their history.

There are people who will say that they saw a great football game Sunday. But they missed the point. What they saw was a drama.

Chapter 1

The Stories Don't Expire

There is a rapid pulse in anyone who gets to retell an Ice Bowl Day experience. More than half a century after the winter clothes closets were raided, the souvenirs collected, the cars jump-started, the digits thawed, and the bets paid, the cast and heirs of the Ice Bowl experience – those in attendance and those attached in other ways – keep their grip on the memories like a birthright.

That is what has sustained the Ice Bowl – the NFL championship football game between the Green Bay Packers and Dallas Cowboys on December 31, 1967 – when a Wisconsin winter served up its most brutal challenge to a sporting community that barely flinched when confronted with such a freezing gauntlet.

The Ice Bowl lives on in barroom conversations, at family reunions, and whenever sports and extreme weather co-mingle to prompt someone to comment or write about "that day back then in Green Bay."

It's the stories that have no expiration date. It's the people, the experiences, and even the scattered memorabilia that have kept the Ice Bowl alive rather than becoming just a footnote in the century-old professional football diary.

It was a day owned and shared by more than the 50,000 who sat and shivered inside Lambeau Field, and by the thousands upon thousands more who have compelling answers to the question: "Where were you during the Ice Bowl?"

No one story captures the full spectrum of that day or that game. While any aging recollection can be prone to exaggeration, Ice Bowl stories seem to survive the tests of time and doubt because they reinforce what was a spirit and a passion that has few comparables in professional sports. These stories add to the image and character of the people and the place where the Ice Bowl happened, and the time it happened.

People still want to talk about it. The media often uses subsequent New Year's Eves to take its readers, listeners, and viewers back to 1967, with the cold weather always the centerpiece and the pride of the storyteller in full view.

It was just one day, one sporting event whose importance paled in comparison to things that really shaped life on Earth back then. But the true story of the Ice Bowl isn't really about football or beastly weather. It's about people who etched memories through an experience that had enough originality to last even beyond their lifetimes. The impact of that day has never left

Green Bay, can never be overemphasized or replaced, and maintains its permanent place on the NFL's shelf of classics.

These are some of the people, some of the stories, about a New Year's Eve day a long time ago. Some stories were shared years ago; some are now being shared by the next generation.

Some storytellers are no longer alive. But the stories are.

Chapter 2

On the Field, Doing Nothing

I had no need to go searching for a first-person perspective of the Ice Bowl. I was there, close up.

I don't remember being cold and I don't remember celebrating. I certainly don't remember anyone suggesting at the time that it would rank among the greatest games ever played, that it would gain legendary status, or that memories and mementoes from that holiday afternoon football game would survive through generations.

Maybe the years and years of telling and retelling people about my experience at that game have dulled the memories. Maybe the brain cells just haven't thawed yet. Maybe the combination of being weaned on Wisconsin winter weather and having happily adjusted to a decade of winning football in Green Bay made the details of that day less dramatic for me at the time. Or maybe my lifetime path that became packed with so many Packers football game experiences just pushed the significance of that one game into a muddle of memories.

I had a job, supposedly, at the Ice Bowl. I've told people I was a part-time reporter at the *Green Bay Press-Gazette* then. Actually, I was still in college and was a part-time sports department clerk who took weekend shifts answering the phone calls from high school coaches who called in their game results. Sports reporting, column writing, editing and a forty-year career in journalism came later.

But the editors farmed me out to the Associated Press for the NFL Championship Game between the Green Bay Packers and Dallas Cowboys on December 31, 1967. It was a simple assignment, to hang out on the side of the field with a photographer who would hand me rolls of film throughout the game that I would carry to some location under the stadium to people who knew what to do with them. I was going to be a runner.

I never did any running. I never saw any rolls of film or located the place where they were supposed to end up. I barely remember the photographer, other than he seemed grumpy and didn't have much to say to me. But before the game began, I noticed him packing his camera equipment into a satchel behind the Packers bench. Something wasn't right. So I asked.

This is Jenny and me on our wedding day, not long after the Ice Bowl.

He said his equipment was frozen and his assignment was ended. When I asked him what he was going to do, he said he was going to the hotel to watch the game, which was doubtful since it was blacked out in Green Bay. When I asked him what I should do, it was apparent that my actions or whereabouts for the next three hours and beyond were not on his list of concerns. He said he could care less what I did. He left and I stayed.

Nobody else down on the field seemed to care what I did either. There was no need to try to look important. So I stood on the sidelines of Lambeau Field at a championship football game with nothing to do, no place to sit, no one to talk to, and without any pressure to act like I belonged there. My field pass indicated I was supposed to stay back against the stands, but it was obvious that nobody of any official status cared where I stood or wanted to do anything about me.

I had a close-up view of what became known as the Ice Bowl and all the drama that unfolded that afternoon. I had a single primary goal: to stay out of the way. The secondary goal was to watch the football game. Somewhere in the list of priorities was likely a desire not to freeze. I don't remember what I was wearing, but being a skier and lifelong resident of Wisconsin, I doubt there was any skin showing.

I walked the sidelines, usually hanging close to the Packers bench, and watched football. I saw the Packers take their 14-0 lead, and watched the Cowboys come back to cut it to 14-10 by halftime. I walked behind the bench when I wanted to follow the game action at the other end of the field. I have a distinct memory of Packers linebacker Ray Nitschke moaning about how cold he was as he tried to get close to a heater near the bench. I didn't try to comfort him.

Halftime was a blur, but I know I never left the field. I was near the Packers bench again when the Cowboys scored a touchdown on the first play of the fourth quarter to go ahead 17-14. From any view, it was clear that the Cowboys were dominating the play on the field.

When the Packers launched their winning drive in the final minutes, I walked the sidelines and found myself at the goal line at the same time they got there. I walked back closer to the Packers bench when quarterback Bart Starr conferred with Coach Vince Lombardi with only sixteen seconds left, and I was back at the goal line when Starr snuck into the end zone and into history. I saw the Cowboys' desperation passes fail and saw people run out on the field to tear down the goal posts. A college friend of mine who had been nursing a flask up in the stands throughout the game found me on the field, although I doubt that he remembers. My girlfriend, soon to be fiancée, was in the care of my family up in the stands. I learned later that she had camped herself in the women's bathroom for parts of the second half.

I didn't stay for the dismantling of the goal posts and didn't leave with any souvenirs. I met my brother at his car and we went home to nearby De Pere. We were clearly aware that the Packers had just won their third straight NFL championship, but like many in the local football culture at that time, nearing borderline spoiled by the team's successes.

I had, by that time, collected several memories of Packers game heroics and would collect more. I was at City Stadium when Gary Knafelc caught that Tobin Rote touchdown pass to beat the Detroit Lions in 1955, when Al Carmichael ran that kickoff back 106 yards against the Chicago Bears in 1956. I saw the Packers beat the Bears in 1957 in the first game at what would later be renamed Lambeau Field, and I remember specifically sitting next to Miss America at that game ... that's another story. I saw the Packers' only victory in the 1958 season, 38-35 over the Philadelphia Eagles. I saw the Packers beat the Bears in Lombardi's first game as head coach in 1959, and again I was on the field, this time in a wheelchair because I had broken my leg in freshman high school football practice.

I was there when they beat the New York Giants 37-0 for the 1961 championship and when they beat the Cleveland Browns in 1965 for another championship. I didn't witness any Packers heroics in the 1970s because there weren't any, unless watching Coach Dan Devine get his leg broken in his first game at Lambeau qualifies. Later, I was at the side of the field when Chester Marcol ran past me with the blocked field goal to score the touchdown to beat the Bears in 1980. I witnessed the playoff victory over the St. Louis Cardinals in 1982, the upset of the Washington Redskins 48-47 in the Monday night game in 1983, and the Snow Bowl victory over Tampa Bay in 1985.

I sat in the press box at Atlanta's Fulton County Stadium that day in 1991 when newly hired general manager Ron Wolf was checking out Falcons backup quarterback Brett Favre for a possible trade, and I was back at Lambeau Field for the conference championship victory over the Carolina Panthers in early 1997 that confirmed Wolf's wisdom in making the trade. I interviewed Barry Sanders after the Packers held him to minus-one yard in the 1995 playoff game, and was just feet away from Yancey Thigpen when he dropped what would have been a game-winning touchdown for the Pittsburgh Steelers at Lambeau Field in a 1995 regular-season game that put the Packers into the playoffs. I watched Al Harris make the pick-six to beat the Seattle Seahawks in the playoff game in 2004, and I watched from the press box at AT&T Stadium in Arlington, Texas, in February 2011 when the Packers beat the Steelers in Super Bowl XLV.

Today, when I tell people of my generation or those slightly younger that I was on the field during the Ice Bowl, they are interested and seemingly impressed. When I tell those much younger, there is usually a need to explain what the Ice Bowl was and why people still talk about it.

The running joke over the decades is that one million people claimed they were at the Ice Bowl, as *Press-Gazette* writer Bob Woessner accurately prophesied two days after the game. I like to respond by saying there were just half a million of us down on the field.

It wasn't just a football game, after all. It was THAT football game when memories – and some toes – became frozen in time. These days, when I step outside and the temperature is around zero, I find an immediate excuse to step back inside. Then I occasionally think about my time at the Ice Bowl and wonder again if I was cold.

I must have been cold. And, like so many who have followed the Packers for so long, I am still celebrating the fact that I was there.

Chapter 3

The Identity Day

A city and its identity are often inseparable. They travel through history together. A city can thrive on its identity or it can try to survive it.

Some community legacies are deserved, for good or bad. Salem, Massachusetts, etched its identity in the seventeenth century when mass hysteria over witchcraft led to trials and executions. Las Vegas created a twentieth century identity with gambling in the desert. Pittsburgh proudly put its face on the steel industry, and New Orleans has reaped the financial benefits from its attachment to jazz slash Mardi Gras slash Cajun slash French Quarter images.

Some cities have no role to play or influence in their connection to an identity. Niagara Falls, New York, even if it wanted, will never escape the image of water – lots of water – going over a cliff. Denver, Colorado, although not in the mountains, will never be able to hide from the shadow of massive peaks or its identity as the gateway to the Rockies. And Carlsbad, New Mexico, has no control over being known as the city near underground caverns where bats live.

Events have pinned identities on other cities, communities, and sites: Gettysburg, Harper's Ferry, Selma, Appomattox, Little Big Horn, Yorktown, Peshtigo, Tombstone, Jamestown, Wounded Knee, Plymouth, Pearl Harbor.

By 1960, Green Bay, Wisconsin, was contentedly and accurately identified both by a paper industry that took advantage of the city's location along a major waterway and its ability to maximize the fruits of its dairyland surroundings through cheesemaking, meatpacking, and food distribution.

There were other signposts that helped pave the path to an identity for the city: its access to vacation destinations such as Door County and the Wisconsin northwoods, and its shipping trade made possible by access to the Great Lakes and the St. Lawrence Seaway. And the community proudly boasted its distinction as a family-friendly, politically conservative, and Catholic-dominated homestead, whose shared stage was a population that also relished its fun, its alcohol – there were 193 establishments in the city with liquor licenses in 1967 – and its sports.

The city's sports calling card was the pro football Green Bay Packers, by then over forty years old. But despite its claim to six championships, what the Packers proffered to the city then was

© Neville Public Museum of Brown County

(From left) Eddie Glick, president of the Packers Alumni, along with Packers Hall of Fame charter members Johnny "Blood" McNally, Verne Lewellen, and Mike Michalske view a display at the newly created Packers Hall of Fame in 1970. (Photo courtesy of the Neville Public Museum of Brown County)

more about its colorful past, colorful characters – names like Lambeau, Blood, Hutson, Hinkle, Herber, Dilweg, Calhoun, Michalske, Lewellen, Canadeo – and unique publicly owned status than it was about modern football accomplishments or memorable moments that future generations could admire and point to in their sports history conversations.

One day changed that and changed it permanently.

December 31, 1967, provided the ingredients that fed the world an iconic symbol to represent and define a city, balanced equally by the forces of supreme cold weather and supreme and dramatic football excellence.

The game that day has its own name – The Ice Bowl.

Its photographic portrayals show a victorious football quarterback lying face down on the ice in an end zone, while unrecognizable human ticket buyers witness it behind clouds of frozen air that had escaped their lungs. The number most associated with that day is -15.

That's what the Ice Bowl means to the generations who have used it to define Green Bay – football and cold. They've seen the film of the game's heroes, cheered the reunions of the performers, and read the stories by people who ranked the game that day as one of the greatest ever. They've read about or seen the collection of souvenirs – pieces of goalposts, benches, ticket stubs, and a Dallas Cowboys warmup jacket – that either left Lambeau Field that day with someone other than who they came in with or weren't supposed to exit the place at all. They've seen pictures of framed ticket stubs, some signed by someone who played in the game. And they talk about the Ice Bowl with adjectives such as "classic" and "legendary" and "historic."

The day before the Packers' victory over the Pittsburgh Steelers in Super Bowl XLV in Dallas in 2011, a breakfast was held in nearby Grapevine to present an award to New Orleans Saints quarterback Drew Brees. Athletes in Action honored Brees for his community service, and the award was in Bart Starr's name.

But the highlight of the event that drew 2,500 people was the presence of Starr and several former Cowboys – Bob Lilly, Rayfield Wright, Leroy Jordan – and several former Packers – Donny Anderson, Chuck Mercein, Jerry Kramer – who played in the Ice Bowl. They shared memories about that frozen day, and its impact was evident among the men.

Now, more than half a century later as of this writing, that New Year's Eve football game has outlasted any other event or trend that society might want to use to attach a definition to Green Bay.

But the impact of December 31, 1967, gained greater and lasting traction because of its timing. It became an iconic event at a time when there was such a craving, a need, for a significant event that didn't include war or ugliness or politics, or even the stressful changes that were swirling around human life at the time.

By the last day of 1967, most people were aware of the tugs and pulls of societal shifts, although it would be months, even years, before the full impact of what was truly a cultural tsunami would be recognized for what it was.

Civil rights was far from turning enough corners thirteen years after the courts mandated desegregation of schools and six years after Freedom Riders began the crusade that motivated Congress to finally pass a voting rights law.

A generation raised in the 1950s was forcing its influence on the way people dressed, behaved, and wore their hair. Drugs were the medicines for rebellion or escape. Sex was more visible, and its treatment in motion pictures challenged traditional social mores. The feminist movement was barely visible on the horizon, but the seeds were being planted.

Music had graduated from the breakthrough of rock 'n' roll over a decade earlier to include folk and protest songs, while the explosion of British bands produced new anthems for a generation.

Nowhere was change more apparent than in the Roman Catholic Church, where the impact of the Second Vatican Council (1962-1965) signaled the faith's arrival to modern times with epic revisions.

Mostly, New Year's Eve 1967 existed at a time of divisive war.

The conflict in Vietnam dominated politics, divided generations and families, and offered debate rather than resolution. And no one could have been fully prepared for the violence that loomed just months ahead in 1968 – assassinations of Martin Luther King Jr. and Robert Kennedy – and the protests and violent summer showdowns at the Democratic National Convention in Chicago.

Change and angst were paired, feeding off each other. So a football game played in ridiculously cold conditions on a playing surface better suited for hockey offered an unusual distraction. It became the seed of folklore to be described, exaggerated, and revisited by those who were part of the story and those who were storytellers.

December 31, 1967.

Chapter 4

7 a.m.-ish and Beyond

The voice from Green Bay radio station WDUZ did its job as Bob Woessner's morning alarm at his village of Allouez home. But it was the greeter's weather report that served as the real wake-up call.

"It's 16 degrees," he said … "below zero."

Not the best encouragement to get out from beneath the covers. But this was a work day for Woessner, a feature writer and columnist at the *Green Bay Press-Gazette*. He had a writing assignment at a championship football game later that day. There would be a press box refuge, of course, but there would also be comfort issues to deal with just to get there, to get to the locker room, and to get back home.

Yes, the radio voice did say 16 degrees below zero. Some people intended to play football that day and so many other people intended to watch them do it.

Three miles to the south in the city of De Pere, JoAnn Hanaway was driving herself to Sunday morning Mass at St. Francis Xavier Catholic Church, while her husband, Don, stayed home with their young children. It was bitter cold, but this was a Sunday and a lifelong Catholic went to church on Sunday. The Hanaways had tickets for the 1 p.m. game.

Forty-five miles farther south, in his University of Wisconsin-Oshkosh dormitory, Mark Thompson had just convinced a college friend to drive him two miles out to Highway 41 so he could try to hitchhike to Green Bay. Thompson's uncle, Guy, had called the previous day and offered a game ticket if Mark could get himself up there. He would rely on his mitten-covered thumb and perhaps a sympathetic traveler to rescue him.

Even farther south, Ted Jones was getting ready to leave his Chicago-area home to drive to Green Bay for the football game. He had obtained a couple game tickets from longtime friend Lynn Mercein, whose husband, Chuck, had been added to the Packers' roster several weeks earlier. Lynn Mercein called Jones early in the morning to say her husband had phoned and given her the grisly forecast. Jones knew Chuck Mercein when they were both at Yale University, so he was prepared to cheer for a Green Bay team despite his Chicago loyalties.

Much, much farther south still, in Buenos Aires, Argentina, De Pere native Cal Lawton woke after the final night of a rest and

Cal Lawton (center) was in a much warmer locale during the Ice Bowl than his family in De Pere. He listened to the game on a transistor radio in Argentina while on an R&R weekend from his Peace Corps duties in Chile. (Photo courtesy of Cal Lawton)

recreation weekend. He and his friends had enjoyed a getaway from their Peace Corps duties in Chile and Lawton had to fly back to Santiago at midday to resume his work with credit co-ops. He knew the timing of his flight threatened his plans to listen to the Packers-Cowboys game on his transistor radio. He also knew that the Argentina weather forecast that day called for a high temperature of 105 degrees ... above zero.

A battery-powered transistor radio would also be Specialist 4 Tyler McCormack's connection to the championship game. Also a De Pere native, McCormack and Sgt. Gary Wayne Cooper, a Dallas native, planned to follow the action on Armed Forces Radio when they stood guard in the middle of the night on a bridge near Chu Lai, Vietnam. Middle of the night in Vietnam was game time in Green Bay.

US Army Specialist 4 Tyler McCormack, a De Pere native, listened to the Ice Bowl on Armed Forces Radio while guarding this bridge in Vietnam along with Sgt. Gary Wayne Cooper of Dallas. (Photo courtesy of Tyler McCormack)

Back in the frozen north, Rob Van Gemert of De Pere was already regretting that he agreed to travel with his brother to Iron Mountain, Michigan, ninety miles north of Green Bay, to spend a Sunday skiing at the Pine Mountain hill. But he would check it out.

Harlan Ihlenfeldt was in a different frame of mind as he went through his daily milking and other chores on his Kewaunee County farm east of Green Bay. His brother, Fred, was taking him to the football game later that day and Harlan, a former lineman for the semi-pro Manitowoc Chiefs, couldn't wait. He had commissioned his daughters, Sharon and Sue, to cut letters for a makeshift sign on a bedsheet that he would take to the game in case there was a chance to display it.

Eleven-year-old Charlie Yeager was up early at his home on Velp Avenue on Green Bay's west side. He walked to the house of his neighbor, Ron, who was a city bus driver. Ron drove them to the city bus garage, where they had time for a quick game of pool before beginning his route to De Pere. Near St. Anne's Episcopal Church on North Broadway, Charlie exited the bus and joined his grandparents and aunt in a pew for Morning Prayer.

Rosemary Petasek had use of her parents' game tickets and wasn't scheduled to work in the surgical post-op unit at St. Mary's Hospital in Green Bay that day. It was hours before game time, but she already had her game wardrobe picked out – leather jacket, mini-skirt and hose, leather boots. She knew enough about the fashion expectations at Packer games, weather be damned.

Arlene Greatens rose early at her town of Eaton home southeast of Green Bay. She heard the weather report, so she began heating some bricks that would find their place at the bottom of the sleeping bag into which she planned to wrap herself when she fulfilled her Packer fan duty at Lambeau Field.

Richard Baldwin, a thirteen-year-old eighth grader in Menomonee Falls, just north of Milwaukee, was getting ready for the drive to Green Bay with his father, Bob. The tickets came to them from friends who were committed to hosting their church's bridge party on New Year's Eve. Bob Baldwin had two Sterno cans that he planned to light to provide warmth, a movie camera to record memories, and a bottle of peppermint schnapps. It would be Richard's first game at Lambeau Field.

Kenneth Eggert was home on leave from the Army. He and his wife, Chris, were making plans to attend morning services at First English Lutheran Church in Oshkosh when they heard a radio report that someone had two free tickets available for the football game in Green Bay. They picked up the tickets and ditched church.

Bob VandeWalle, in his second year at the US Naval Academy in Annapolis, was home on leave in De Pere and just waking up from a short night's sleep. He and friends had lingered into the wee hours at the Club 18 and Danny's Pizza Garden, finally calling it a morning at 3 a.m. Now twenty years old and charting his own life course, VandeWalle nevertheless was spending his leave at his parents' house, and the house rules dictated that the family goes to church Sunday morning regardless of age, weather, or previous night's activities. So VandeWalle was set to go to Mass with the family, then the game, all the while thinking about the money he hoped to make from academy classmates who placed bets on the Cowboys. He was still basking in the memory of what he collected from fellow cadets when the Packers won the 1966 title, and would collect from those who put money on the Los Angeles Rams a week earlier when the Packers beat them.

Seventeen-year-old Steve Kerkes had no plans to spend part of his day sitting in a frozen stadium. He was committed to his Sunday job as a busboy at the Oneida Country Club on Green Bay's far west side. He had morning duties at the club and was also scheduled to work at the New Year's Eve social later.

Jim Parish's day was planned around a session of Sheepshead with several friends at the Prom, a beer hangout in West De Pere. He and his friends would keep tabs on the game from there.

Jim Buchholz had work assignments at WLUK-TV just east of the stadium, where he had been hired as a part-time cameraman. His first task would be to set up about forty chairs in the station studio for the company's top advertisers who were invited to come to watch the championship game – which was blacked out in Green Bay. It was to be secretly streamed in from its sister station in Marquette, Michigan.

Tere Duperrault, a high school junior living with relatives in their home south of De Pere, was rummaging through her wardrobe to find warm clothes. The Packer games were always on her calendar, and she was set to go with her Aunt Dottie and Uncle Ralph, and their three sons.

Jane Switzer wasn't planning to go to the game since her husband, John, a trainman for Green Bay & Western Railroad, was on the road in Wisconsin Rapids, and she had a toddler at home. But she and her sister heard on the radio that an elderly lady in Allouez would sell her tickets to the first person that came to her door. To pursue, or not to pursue.

Kate Sorensen, a sophomore at St. Norbert College in De Pere, wasn't looking forward to her job working a frigid concession stand at Lambeau Field, but she and her twin sister, Karen, would go anyway.

Kate's boyfriend, Pete Sabel, was home on leave from Fort Campbell, Kentucky, where he was two weeks into his basic training. He left the University of Wisconsin two months earlier after the Dow Chemical protests and enlisted. Sabel suddenly found himself with a ticket for the game. His brother, Jim, having checked the weather forecast early in the morning, decided that visiting a girlfriend in Fond du Lac had better New Year's Eve potential than sitting in an arctic football stadium. For Pete, there would be a game to attend, then a New Year's Eve party, then an early morning bus back to Kentucky.

Paul Minten, living in West De Pere, was fifteen but had already advanced from selling hot dogs at Lambeau Field to the better-selling peanuts concession. He would find out later if there was a market for peanuts at the championship game when potential buyers would have to remove their gloves or mittens to fumble for change.

Bruce Mommaerts, a fifteen-year-old sophomore at Green Bay Southwest High School, was preparing to fulfill the $20 job he acquired through Manpower Inc. He and his school friends, Art Attala and Gary McFarland, would go to the stadium and do whatever tasks the Proski team required. Bruce's mother was already getting him ready for the cold. She showed him how to put bread bags between the cotton and wool sock layers on his feet to keep his toes from freezing. Bruce got his father's World War II army coat out of the closet and the thick Mickey Mouse boots. He would be ready.

Joe Bowers of Appleton, who was playing football for the semi-pro Manitowoc Chiefs, had his own ambitious plans. He had a part-time job in the camera department of the H.C. Prange Company, and he wanted to see if he could finagle his way onto the field at Lambeau and take some pictures during the game. He had a ticket, but he planned to bring a camera with him to see if he could get to the field level at some point. It would require some creative maneuvering, he decided.

Patti Kramer, a nineteen-year-old clerk at the Banta Company in Menasha, decided to surprise her mother, Alice, a huge Packers fan who had never attended a game. Patti had a friend in Oshkosh who wasn't going to use his two tickets, and offered them to her for free. She told her mother to get dressed for a football game.

Ray Barrington was ten years old and living in rural Hortonville, southwest of Green Bay. His mother worked for a law firm in Appleton and was given tickets for the game, but she worried about the effects of the frigid temperatures on her son. She decided they would give it a try and see how long he could last.

Pam Duebler, a high school student in Manitowoc, was still basking in the glow of the Christmas Day moment when she was able to surprise her father, Chester, with two $12 tickets to the championship football game. The tickets became available from a school friend's family, and Pam got her mother's approval to use her allowance and some babysitting money to buy them. Her Dad, a foreman at Mirro Aluminum and a big Packers fan, teared up when he saw the tickets.

Jim Killinger, a Nebraska native who had just begun his dental practice in Oshkosh three months earlier, had accepted an invitation from another dentist to accompany him to what would be his first Packers game that day. He was curious to see what Packers football, and Wisconsin weather, were all about.

Joe Jarosh, back home in Manitowoc during the UW-La Crosse holiday break, was persuaded to join friends for the drive to Green Bay and the game, even though he wasn't really a Packers fan.

Susan Creviere (a.k.a. Sister Margaret Mary) didn't have the Packers or a championship game on her radar. Her life as a cloistered novice consisted of cozy comfort and devotions at Our Lady of Charities convent about two miles west of the stadium. It was time for the morning prayers.

Tom Hinz was a first-year police officer in Green Bay and knew he'd be assigned to stairwell security between sections 8 and 10 at Lambeau Field, where he used to work as an usher. He also knew there would probably be a traffic control assignment near the stadium after the game.

Brad Nuss was home from college and was already chatting with friends about trying to sneak into the game. The stadium was rimmed by a ten-foot chain link fence ... very surmountable if security teams could be avoided.

Steve Seidl, home for the holiday break from Marquette University, worked with his father, Len, to make sure they could counter the cold. They packed charcoal into an empty one-pound coffee can, then soaked it with lighter fluid. If the toes got cold enough at the game, they reasoned, they would light the coals, cover the can with an army blanket and warm their feet as they sat in their seats at Lambeau Field.

The Weiss family from Eau Claire in western Wisconsin, all seven of them, was waking up at the Valley Motel on nearby Military Avenue. They had their usual tickets for Section 129 and sixteen-year-old Joe Weiss had his Norelco tape recorder. He planned to take it to the stadium, pretend he was broadcasting over a fictitious radio station, and do a play-by-play throughout the game.

Rocky Bleier, the former Appleton Xavier football star who captained the Notre Dame football team in 1967, was six weeks removed from the ligament injury he sustained against Georgia Tech. Home for the holiday, he decided to accompany his father to the game at Lambeau Field. This meant taking off the removable cast, and putting layers of clothes around the left knee. He would have to use crutches to get to and from his seat.

The preambles for Ice Bowl stories were in place.

Chapter 5

A Welcome Mood Changer

If a football game in cold weather was going to be significant enough to invite adjectives such as iconic, legendary and historic, it required some context to be fully appreciated and credited.

The Ice Bowl shared its place in history with events and trends that made the sporting event along what was then Highland Avenue (later Lombardi Avenue) a very welcome intrusion. The game stood out not only because of what happened, but when it happened, and what else was competing for space in the human mind at the time.

History would record the 1960s as a time of change, of turmoil, of rebellion, and of war. And while the last day of 1967 saw the end of a year where tension thrived, it also would prove to be a time that ushered in a year when the embers of violence would billow.

It was a time when the country, according to *New York Times* writer James Reston, "was yearning for unity and purpose." The National Committee for an Effective Congress issued a report that stated "the country may now be on the brink of a third trauma, a depression of the national spirit."

The war in Vietnam hogged the front pages and television news cycles. But there was little resolution by December 31, 1967. General William Westmoreland, the military chieftain, was on record at year's end saying, "We have reached an important point when the end begins to come into view," but the view from any vantage point wasn't clear and hardly optimistic. The battles in Asia were countered by increasing numbers of protests in the United States.

It led to ugliness and divisiveness. Lt. Gen. Lewis Hershey, the Selective Service director, ordered draft boards to draft war protestors. Joseph Califano Jr., special assistant to President Lyndon Johnson, went before a congressional committee days before the Ice Bowl to talk back Hershey's directive, spurred no doubt by a frantic letter signed by the presidents of eight Ivy League colleges. The courts eventually nullified Hershey's order, but it prompted a sharp increase in the number of burned draft cards.

Four U.S. Navy sailors jumped ship in Japan and sought asylum in Sweden, saying they took their drastic step to protest the war.

Violent confrontations involving students and police had occurred in Madison two months earlier when Dow Chemical, makers of napalm, tried to resume its job recruitment on the University of Wisconsin campus. It put Wisconsin at the center of the antiwar movement.

The war had become a political lynchpin by late 1967. Minnesota Sen. Eugene McCarthy, a Democrat, parted ways with President Johnson's administration because of the war. It was just days before the Ice Bowl when McCarthy said he would enter the Wisconsin Presidential Primary election in April 1968, a direct challenge to the country's leadership at the time.

Defense Secretary Robert McNamara resigned in November to become president of World Bank after Johnson rejected his recommendation that the United States freeze its troop levels in Vietnam and stop bombing North Vietnam. And Martin Luther King Jr. had denounced the war earlier in the year.

There was a stunning medical breakthrough in the weeks prior to the Ice Bowl. South African surgeon Christian Barnard performed the world's first heart transplant. His patient survived the surgery but died weeks later from pneumonia, and Barnard was preparing to perform a second surgery early in 1968. It marked a major breakthrough in medical history.

Racial tension remained high and events in Wisconsin contributed to it. There were riots in Milwaukee as Fr. James Groppi spearheaded a move to overcome housing restrictions for African Americans in the city. And devastating racial riots dominated the summer of 1967 in Detroit and Newark. At the same time, the United States Supreme Court ruled that bans on interracial marriages were unconstitutional, and Thurgood Marshall became the first Black named to the high court.

Tragedy didn't take the year off, either. Three astronauts – Virgil (Gus) Grissom, Ed White, and Roger Chaffee – died when a flash fire broke out in their spacecraft while it was on the ground at Cape Kennedy. And nine girls from the small city of Juda in southern Wisconsin perished when a plane crashed into the New Orleans hotel where they were staying during a senior class trip.

The year saw the establishment of the National Transportation Safety Board after Ralph Nader's book, *Unsafe at Any Speed,* exposed the dangers on the nation's highways and in the automobile industry.

It was the height of the Beatles' popularity. They produced the most popular song of the year, *All You Need is Love,* and the album that would become their trademark, *Sgt. Pepper's Lonely Hearts Club Band.* Another popular musician in 1967 was Johnny Rivers for his hit song, *Baby, I Need Your Loving.* And the youth were also drawn to Jim Morrison and The Doors, who produced the song that would resonate with a generation, *Light My Fire.*

Fitting the times, the new musical *Hair* opened off-Broadway the month before the Ice Bowl.

Hollywood produced many movies in 1967 that would become classics: *The Graduate, Bonnie and Clyde, Cool Hand Luke, To Sir, With Love, Guess Who's Coming to Dinner,* and *The Dirty Dozen.* And the most popular TV shows during the year were *The Fugitive* and *The Monkees.*

The fashion trend of the year was impacted by an English model named Twiggy. And a new magazine – *Rolling Stone* – published its first issue six weeks before the Ice Bowl.

In sports, U.S. Open golf champion Jack Nicklaus was the tour's top money winner at $188,998, and UCLA won the first of its seven consecutive NCAA basketball titles. The Associated Press athletes of the year were Carl Yastrzemski of the Boston Red Sox and tennis champion Billie Jean King.

The national spirit was the theme of a *Press-Gazette* editorial writer who looked ahead to 1968 with little regret about leaving 1967:

> *"The symptoms are there for all of us to see but exactly what sort of an illness they proclaim is more difficult to determine.*

> *"There is the widespread dissent over the war and the inability of anyone to explain satisfactorily why we are so involved. There is unrest in our cities and so far no solutions before the next hot summer.*

> *"There is growing racial strife, a hardening of opinion on all sides, an increase in calls for violence by both black and white.*

"There is the 'new morality' which is interpreted by some to be no morality at all, the appalling growth of drug addiction, what appears to be a drive toward self destruction ... and the frustrations and the lack of identity for the individual American."

It was the tone, it was the mood, it was the temper of life as dawn broke on December 31, 1967.

But, cold or not, it was a perfect Green Bay time for a football game.

Chapter 6

10 a.m.-ish and Beyond

It wasn't the welcome home that JoAnne Hanaway expected when she entered her front door after church. The screams came from her two-year-old daughter, Maureen, who had just had her right thumb slammed in a door when she was chasing her brother. JoAnne and Don Hanaway would spend the next couple hours in the St. Vincent Hospital emergency room while Dr. Bruce Stoehr tended to the injury. Clearly, they would be late for the game, but there was also the question of whether they should leave the wounded child with a babysitter.

Two-year-old Maureen Hanaway and her mother, JoAnn, pose for a 1967 Christmas season photo a week before the Ice Bowl. (Photo courtesy of JoAnn Hanaway)

Hitchhiking in severe cold wasn't Mark Thompson's great desire, but it seemed to be his only option if he was going to get from Oshkosh to Green Bay for that football game. The fact that he seemed to be the only one doing it that morning probably worked in his favor. A Wisconsin State Trooper who was patrolling along Highway 41 in Oshkosh that morning, most likely checking for stalled vehicles, spotted Thompson and pulled over. He got right to the point.

"What are you doing?" he asked. Told of the young man's intent to get to Green Bay, the trooper, perhaps not wanting to contribute to a body being frozen along the highway during his watch, told him to hop in. He drove Thompson forty miles to Oneida Street in Ashwaubenon, just south of Lambeau Field, never notifying his superiors that he had a passenger.

The 170-member University of Wisconsin-La Crosse marching band, the Marching Chiefs, took the field at the empty stadium to run through the thirteen-minute routine they were scheduled to perform at halftime of the game. The practice session became traumatic.

As soon as the session concluded, twelve of the band members had to be rushed to St. Mary's Hospital and treated for exposure. Band director Ralph Wahl went into conference with doctors and Packers officials, and decided that the halftime show had to be cancelled. Keeping his band outside for an hour, with the students' lips touching metal mouthpieces and the fingers exposed on clarinets and flutes, couldn't be justified.

Bruce Mommaerts and his friends showed up for the work crew at the stadium and were told to help roll the heavy tarp off the field. Right away, they noticed the steam rising from the electric wire system under the field. A supervisor then instructed Bruce to get a broom and sweep ice and snow off the NFL emblem at the 20-yard line.

In Hortonville, southwest of Green Bay, ten-year-old Ray Barrington waited for his mother to finally decide if they would use those game tickets given to her by her employer. When she decided to do it, Ray got ready. It involved long underwear, sweat pants, snow pants, plastic bags over the feet, and boots.

His brother's game ticket in hand, Pete Sabel called his friend, Tim McDonough, to see if he could hitch a ride to the game with him and his father. Request approved.

Following church, Charlie Yeager had breakfast at his grandparents' home. Then his Aunt Marion drove him and his twelve-year-old cousin, Jeff, back to Charlie's home. His father, Bob, was waiting to take them to the WLUK-TV station where he worked and had to set up chairs for the people who would watch the game when it was streamed in from Marquette, Michigan. Charlie and Jeff watched every home game at the station.

Patti Kramer and her mother, Alice, put on their snowmobile suits and heavy socks. Patti's father, Ned, cut up cardboard boxes that would provide a place beneath their feet and protection from the ice-cold bench.

Peter Helf and David Martin, both twenty-two, parked their car near the Brown County Veterans Memorial Arena east of the stadium. They had all-access passes for the game because they would be delivering food from the Proski concessions to the referees and other game officials. Fortified with bottles of schnapps, they had to walk backwards up to Lambeau Field because of the cold wind.

The Lambeau Field grounds crew, under the direction of John Proski, pulls the icy tarp off the field. (Photo courtesy of the Neville Public Museum of Brown County)

Jane Switzer and her sister, Kitty, decided they would drive to St. Mary's Boulevard in Allouez and see if that elderly lady still had those tickets she wasn't going to use. A five-minute drive later and they had the tickets in hand. Jane decided to wear her fashion boots to the game.

Dick Egan, a native of De Pere now living in Allouez, returned home with his wife, Annie, after attending morning Mass at the St. Norbert Abbey. By then, it was apparent that the outdoor temperature was more severe than had been forecast. Annie Egan announced that she wasn't going to the game, but her husband decided to call the National Weather Service for advice. The meteorologist who answered the phone had a ready reply: Don't go to the game. Egan decided to bundle up anyway. He knew it was too late to find a buyer for his wife's ticket and headed for the stadium.

Kenneth and Chris Eggert, of Oshkosh, arrived at Lambeau Field with their free tickets in hand. Immediately, they ran into a couple who were offering to pay $20 and trade their end zone tickets to anyone who had seats closer to the middle of the field. The Eggerts grabbed them.

Frank Steffel, a sixteen-year-old high school junior, had plans to make the best of things despite the cold wave. He and some friends bought six-packs of beer that they planned to smuggle under their jackets. Perhaps they'd drink one of the beers before they got there. Legal beer-drinking age was eighteen in Wisconsin, but for many that was just a recommendation.

Michael Lefebvre joined some St. Norbert College fraternity brothers for their regular fundraising gig of selling beer for the Proski concessions. They showed up to see if it would be worthwhile.

Steve Kerkes arrived at Oneida Golf and Riding Club, and prepared to help set tables. A married couple, members of the club, showed up and announced they had no interest in going to the football game. They gave their tickets to Kerkes and a co-worker at no charge.

Bob VandeWalle, the Midshipman, put his wardrobe together. Hunting clothes, boots, two pair of wool socks, long underwear, his Navy peacoat and watch cap, flannel shirt, sweater, and a pair of borrowed gloves.

Jay Erbeck, on leave from his Marine Corps duties at Glenview Naval Air Station near Chicago where he repaired helicopters, had more on his mind than the football game. He went to pick up his fiancée, West De Pere High School home economics teacher Kathleen Berens, to take her to the game. They were get-

Jay Erbeck and his fiancée, Kathleen Berens, prepare to drive to Lambeau Field for the game. (Photo courtesy of Jay Erbeck)

ting ready to mail the invitations for their February wedding.

Jim Buchholz arrived at WLUK-TV so he could set up those chairs for guests who would watch the game that was set to be streamed in from Marquette. A US Marshall met him at the door and informed him that only employees would be permitted inside that day. Buchholz told the marshall that he had to set up chairs, but the official told him that nobody would be coming to watch a game. Apparently, someone at the Green Bay CBS affiliate had filed a complaint. The competing station would be showing the

While Cal Lawton was nice and warm in Buenes Aires, preparing to return to his Peace Corps duties in Chile, his family was getting bundled up to attend the Ice Bowl with friends. Among those pictured are Cal's father, Charles (Choppy) in the back right, his mother, Marian (front center), and sister, Barbara (front left). (Photo courtesy of Cal Lawton)

game in full the following day.

Ron Fassbender, who had just taken a job with the Wisconsin Conservation Department in western Wisconsin, was at his parents' home on Ridge Road just south of the stadium and was primed for the game. His brother, Bob, called from his job at Green Bay Aviation at Austin Straubel Field with a tempting offer. Some private jets from Texas brought Cowboy fans to Green

Bay for the game and some were looking for tickets. Ron and his brother could make a healthy profit if they wanted to sell theirs. They were hearing numbers of around $350 apiece floated their way.

Fassbender's mother told Ron he would be crazy not to sell the tickets. He chose cold and crazy, and turned down the offer.

Cal Lawton had his next few hours planned. Still at his hotel in Buenes Aires, he would catch a cab to the airport and then listen to the game on his large transistor radio before his flight to Santiago. Armed Forces Radio would have the game on, and with any luck, he could hear the entire game before his flight took off.

Kate Sorensen and her twin sister, Karen, showed up at the stadium and prepared to work their assigned Proski concession stand. Cooking hamburgers would be part of the day's assignment, an interesting challenge.

Brad Nuss's high school graduation portrait, taken about two years before the Ice Bowl. (Photo courtesy of Brad Nuss)

Fifteen-year-old Paul Minten was finishing his third season selling food at the stadium. His father dropped him and friends at the stadium by 10:30. He had started out selling hot dogs the first year, when he earned a nickel for every 25-cent hot dog sold, but preferred the peanuts concession. They sold for 15 cents a bag and he collected three cents per sale, but they were more popular among the fans so he made more money.

On this morning, however, Minten knew nobody was going to remove mittens or gloves to buy peanuts. So, after checking in at the stadium, he just started walking around. He saw groundskeepers beginning to remove the tarp covering the field and, with no security preventing him, Minten walked down to the field and helped roll the tarp. That completed, he surmised that the field would be the best place to watch the game, so he found a spot in the southeast corner near the end zone and sat.

Bob and Richard Baldwin found their seats twenty rows up in the northwest corner of the stadium. The frigid air made it impossible to light the Sterno cans, and the movie camera froze before they could record anything of value. The peppermint schnapps, however, survived and Richard got his first taste of it.

Bob Woessner reported to the press box and found out that he didn't have an assigned seat. Fortunately, the press box manager was *Press-Gazette* pressman Clem Collard, who found Woessner a place to stand near the back of the box.

Brad Nuss, the twenty-year-old college student home in De Pere during the holidays, had already decided that the best way to see the game was sneaking in rather than driving someplace where it wasn't blacked out. He recruited his brother, Ladd, and friend, Dick Rifleman. They piled into Rifleman's Volkswagen and surveyed the stadium perimeter for the best place to enter Lambeau Field. Fortunately for them, the hurdle into the stadium was just a seven-foot chain link fence with three strands of barbed wire draped across the top. They parked the car and looked for an opportunity.

At the southeast corner of the stadium, they noticed a pair of fourteen-year-old boys who had the same idea. One of the boys had already scaled the fence and was inside, but the other had his pants leg hooked on the wire. The security guards nearby were occupied in helping an ambulance exit the south gate, so Brad and Ladd helped free the boy and managed to climb over themselves. A rushing security guard stopped Rifleman from joining them … temporarily. He subsequently ran into a priest who had been one of his teachers at Abbot Pennings High School in De Pere, and who had an extra ticket. Rifleman, now in the stadium legally, rejoined his friends inside Lambeau Field.

Paul Casanova, a Green Bay East jayvee basketball player, had planned to get into the stadium his usual way: put on tennis shoes and climb the I-beam that enabled him to get over the fence to the top off the men's restroom. But when he arrived at the stadium, he discovered that nobody was taking tickets at one of the gates, and he just walked in.

Keith Budzis, a twenty-one-year-old gas station attendant, was already looking ahead to a possible Packers victory and what he figured would produce a dismantling of the goalposts. So he contacted his friend, Bill Boyea, and they hatched a plan. They would borrow a couple acetylene torches from a friend's garage on the city's east side and have it available to cut up goalposts if the opportunity arose. They would leave the torches in Budzis's 1963 Chevrolet convertible until they were needed, and take their seats in Section 14.

Ken and Ed Vanderloop were veteran beer sellers between Sections 32 and 34. They got ready to walk the steps to find out if their usual customers wanted a cold one on a cold day.

Chapter 7

Community Mayhem

Football shaped the schedules and controlled Northeastern Wisconsin minds the week prior to the Ice Bowl, but there was grist for other conversations.

Some possibly talked about a report indicating that illegitimate births in the country had tripled since 1940. Or that the US Department of Agriculture predicted that cigarette consumption in 1968 was expected to exceed the record 552 billion smokes by Americans in 1967 and 41 billion more than in 1964 when the government issued its warning about a connection between smoking and cancer.

No doubt, a report from the Institute for Sex Research at Indiana University made the rounds at coffee tables during the week. It concluded that there has been no sexual revolution. The study, conducted with 1,200 college students, concluded that women still equate their first sexual experience with love.

Said Dr. Paul Gebhard, the director: "All this sounds like a continuation of the trend toward sexual equality with the female being regarded by males and herself as less a sexual object to be exploited and more as a fellow human with her own needs, expectations and rights."

Some notice was given to the arrest of six Green Bay boys and men, ages fourteen to twenty, who finally admitted to fourteen burglaries, including the theft of a $3,000 coin collection at Packerland Packing Company, after the fathers of two of the youths turned them in.

Newspaper readers learned that twenty-one-year-old Harry Hebard, who was accused of killing five members of his west side Green Bay family nearly five years earlier, pled innocent by reason of insanity.

There was continuing news in the Catholic Diocese of Green Bay four weeks after the death of Bishop Stanislaw Bona, who had served in that role for more than twenty years. Leaders of the 250-member Priests Association of the Green Bay Diocese asked to have a voice in the selection of Bona's successor.

There were movies to attend. The Bay Theater was finishing its second week headlining *To Sir, With Love* starring Sidney Poitier. The West Theater had the light-hearted *Thoroughly Modern Millie* with Julie Andrews. The De Pere Theater had its turn with *Grand Prix* starring James Garner. The Vic Theater in downtown

Green Bay closed up *The Ambushers* with Dean Martin and was getting ready for the New Year's Eve debut of *Valley of the Dolls*.

None of the theaters had yet featured the new movie hit *The Graduate*, which just debuted nationally in early December.

The greater Green Bay community was doing what it had become accustomed to in the Lombardi decade: putting football championship preparation high on agendas. As one *Green Bay Press-Gazette* reporter wrote as Ice Bowl Week commenced, "the formula for community mayhem is brewing."

The Sports Committee of the Greater Green Bay Area Chamber of Commerce jumped right in with Phase 2 of its "Go, Pack, Go. Go All the Way" campaign, following the first phase that preceded the divisional title showdown against the Los Angeles Rams on December 23. The committee, nicknamed the Minutemen, was comprised of many civic leaders including *Press-Gazette* publisher Dan Beisel and three members of his sports department – Art Daley, Lee Remmel and Len Wagner. It also included former Packers Bernard Darling and John Martinkovic, TV personalities Al Sampson, Jim Irwin and Bob Schulze, businessmen Al Schneider, Carl Witteborg and Paul Mazzoleni, St. Norbert College president Rev. Dennis Burke, and Dr. George Nadeau.

"We wanted to rekindle the fans' spirit to assist the Packers in their drive to their second Super Bowl appearance," the committee announced in a published statement. "The goal of the program was to take advantage of the tremendous national exposure resulting from these games in selling the state of Wisconsin, Packerland, and Green Bay, as the place to live, work and play."

It urged fans to participate in a four-part booster campaign by sending victory messages to a mailbox number (that would be made available to the team), wear Packers colors all week, and decorate store windows with Packers themes. It also asked fans to display the American flag without indicating what that had to do with the Packers.

The committee distributed 50,000 bumper stickers and 50,000 banners with the Sure Way, Red Owl and SuperValu grocery stores serving as distribution centers.

Boy Scouts were enlisted to stencil "Go, Pack, Go" stickers on the front windows of Green Bay stores and businesses. A service station scheduled to be torn down at the corner of Dousman and Maple streets on the city's west side was repainted in bright green and gold with victory messages painted in two-foot-high letters. It included a game prediction: Packers 40, Cowboys 17.

The historic Beaumont Hotel was booked to capacity for the New Year's weekend, as were the Holiday Inn in nearby Ashwaubenon and the Downtowner Motel in Green Bay. The forty-year-old Northland Hotel served as the National Football League headquarters for the week.

Five days before the Ice Bowl, Packers ticket director Merrill Knowlton said the game was virtually assured of being a sellout. He said there was a very slight possibility of a few more tickets becoming available later in the week if other NFL teams decided to return their allotments. Nevertheless, the game would be blacked out on television sets in the Green Bay and Wausau viewing areas, per the terms of the TV contract.

Some of the usual banter between city officials was at play early in the week. Green Bay mayor Don Tilleman proposed a friendly wager to Dallas mayor Erik Jonsson, offering a thirty-pound

Green Bay mayor Don Tilleman (center) examines a block of cheese that was part of his friendly wager with Dallas mayor Erik Jonsson. With Tilleman are Al Schneider (left), chairman of the Green Bay Chamber of Commerce's sports committee, and Steve Suidzinski (right), president of Steve's Cheese. (Photo courtesy of the Neville Public Museum of Brown County)

block of cheese and some paper products as Green Bay's stake. Jonsson replied by offering to send some Texas black-eyed peas, informing Tilleman that the peas would be sent immediately after the first of the year if the Cowboys lost.

"If consumed on the first day of the year it insures, as the legend says, good luck throughout the year," Jonsson wrote. "Wouldn't be the same if delivered Dec. 31, you understand."

The Packers returned to practice at Lambeau Field on December 26, but only after some ice-breaking occurred. Custodian John Proski had his crew drive jeeps over the tarps to break up the ice that had gathered on top of them. Proski noted that despite the zero temperature, the turf registered at 50 degrees and would, he said, be at that temperature for the Sunday game.

Lombardi met with the media four days before the Ice Bowl and talked about the electric heating system that had been installed before the season.

"It's beautiful," he said. "This is our first year with the system, of course, so we find a flaw here, and a flaw there. We have discovered certain parts of the field to have more heat than others because of how the sun and the wind strike it.

"We'll have to make adjustments after the season is over. We can't make any changes now. We can make one section warmer the way the system is presently set up, but not beyond that. However, you can use cleats, and it's going to be a fast field."

Lombardi gave the visiting Dallas media a tour of the controlling equipment for the electric blanket that was expected to keep the field from freezing up. He also gave thanks to John Harrington, the field engineer, for the success of the electric blanket.

On the same day, Dallas publicity director Curt Mosher told Green Bay media that the Cowboys decided to stay home to practice rather than trying to adapt to the northern weather. He admitted that if the Rams had beaten the Packers in the playoff game, the Cowboys would have already travelled to Santa Barbara to get ready for the game.

Western Union announced it would install 20 to 30 circuits underneath the stadium – moving them from the press box – to facilitate the transmission of newspaper copy. The expectation was that more than 250,000 words would need to be sent during and after the game.

A unique system was planned. When a writer wanted to send copy, he would raise his hand and the paper would be collected by a messenger. The plan was to put the paper in a pouch and then lower it out the back of the press box on a fishing line to another messenger on the ground, who would take it under the stadium to be transmitted.

Controversy of another kind stirred two days before the game when *Press-Gazette* reporter Carolyn Stewart tried to get a field pass or press box pass for the game. The league informed her that women weren't issued such passes.

Said NFL publicity director Jim Kensil: "We don't want anything to happen to women on the field."

When NFL Commissioner Pete Rozelle held a Friday morning press conference at the Northland Hotel, Stewart attended and asked him about the rule.

"We like women too much for that," he said.

Stewart said she would take her seat in the stands and might stand through the entire game since she wasn't allowed to stand on the field.

Rozelle turned his attention to the issue of free agency, where players become free agents after their contracts expire. The Packers' Jim Taylor did it after the 1965 season when he left to play for the New Orleans Saints, forcing Rozelle to intercede and work out a compromise where the Packers received the Saints' first-round draft choice.

"If this becomes widespread, it could severely hurt pro football," Rozelle told the gathered media in Green Bay. "There's blacklisting, but I won't permit it. We can't have that. But we do feel compensation can solve it. That way the club losing a player gets something in return."

Green Bay Press-Gazette reporters Sarah Alden (left) and Carolyn Stewart (center) carry signs protesting the NFL's policy denying field passes or press box passes for female reporters. (Photo courtesy of the Neville Public Museum of Brown County)

Rozelle promptly left Green Bay to fly to the West Coast, where he planned to attend the Oakland Raiders vs. Houston Oilers game to decide the American Football League title instead of the Packers-Cowboys game.

The *Press-Gazette* put its confidence in the Packers on display with an editorial two days before the Ice Bowl.

> *"As they approach their biggest 1967 challenge Sunday, the Packers can be assured that their supporters in Green Bay and throughout Wisconsin as well as millions of others throughout the nation know that they will meet the challenge with everything they have in skill, prowess and determination to retain the league crown."*

Oblivious to most fans was the financial breakdown of the upcoming championship game. The NFL informed the teams that the total radio and television receipts for the game would be $2 million. Of that, $975,000 would go to a fund for player benefits and pension, $200,000 would go to the league office, and 70 percent of the remaining $825,000 would go to the competing teams, the winner getting 60 percent and the loser 40 percent. Some money would also be distributed to other NFL teams that finished high in their divisions.

The Cowboys were scheduled to fly into the Appleton airport on Friday, two days before the game, since they were to be staying at the Holiday Inn on Highway 41 on Appleton's west side. Then Russ Skall, who operated a supper club in Appleton, received a phone call from Gil Brandt, the Cowboys' promotions director. Skall and Brandt had attended Notre Dame University together. Brandt told him that the Cowboys' flight was being redirected to Austin Straubel Airport in Green Bay.

Skall contacted Appleton mayor George Buckley and city council president John Ayers, and the three men drove to Green Bay to be part of the welcoming committee. The seventy-two-member Dallas contingent poured into two chartered buses for the trip down to Appleton. But Buckley decided to have the bus carrying the players take a circuitous route so he could show off his city. The bus driver left Highway 41 at Ballard Road, turned on Wisconsin Avenue, and then on to Meade Street, finally traveling through the major business district of College Avenue with a police escort and sirens blaring.

Members of the Dallas media who had arrived at the Holiday Inn on the other bus wondered what happened to the team, but Buckley explained.

"Oh, we sort of detoured them so they could get a look at our million dollar College Avenue," the mayor said. It was noted that Buckley was running for re-election in the spring of 1968.

While Dallas officials were having dinner at Skall's restaurant that evening, some of the players welcomed reporters into their motel rooms for brief interviews. The weather was a common topic.

Linebacker LeeRoy Jordan downplayed the cold.

"We have been practicing in temperatures in the low thirties, and we even had snow," Jordan said. "We thought Landry ordered it special so we could get used to handling a wet and slippery ball."

Defensive tackle Bob Lilly expressed the same sentiment.

"We had it cold at home and it shouldn't make any difference," he said.

Quarterback Don Meredith just focused on his team's chances against the Packers as he talked to *Press-Gazette* reporter Jim Zima.

"We have an excellent chance to win," he said. "We are confident and it just remains to be seen if we can execute well. To beat the Packers, you have to out-execute them, and this is the thing we have to go out and do."

Although a second trip to the Super Bowl was still not assured, ninety-three people had already booked reservations to fly to Miami on a charter flight as part of a two-night package arranged by the chamber. A second charter would be arranged in case the Packers beat Dallas. Travelers would have the option of booking a five-night trip that included a couple nights in the Bahamas in addition to the game.

Both teams took limbering-up sessions on the Lambeau Field turf the day before the game – the Packers at 10 a.m., the Cowboys at noon. The overall opinion was that the field was in good shape and the Cowboys said they would plan to wear their regular cleats.

In all, eighty-five writers were expected to be in attendance for the game, with the total media attendance – equipment personnel and staff – exceeding 400.

Most of Green Bay went about its usual holiday weekend routine. More than 1,900 packed into the Brown County Veterans Memorial Arena to watch the Green Bay Bobcats hockey team beat the Marquette Iron Rangers 2-0.

By late in the week, the weather began to become an issue, but Cy Ulsperger of the US Weather Bureau at Austin Straubel Field wasn't ready to make a bold prediction.

"If we start forecasting too far in advance, it might bust wide open with a bright sunny day," he noted. He said Green Bay was caught in a circulating system coming from the Canadian provinces, with a lot of cold air and no interruption in sight.

Still, forty-eight hours before game time, the prediction was for temperatures in the mid to high teens at kickoff. Above zero.

The thermometer dropped to minus-8 in the early morning hours of Friday, December 29, but was up to plus-16 by midnight Friday, reached plus-18 two hours later, and stayed in the teens throughout the day Saturday. In fact, it was plus-13 at 9 p.m. Saturday.

Dallas Cowboys quarterback Don Meredith meets with reporters in his room at the Holiday Inn in Appleton the Friday evening before the game. (Photo courtesy of the Neville Public Museum of Brown County)

Then, it got colder steadily. By midnight, it was plus-6 and by 3 a.m. it was zero. Three hours later, the temperature dropped to minus-9, and as much of the community – and the players – stirred at 7 a.m., it was minus-12. Two hours later, the Green Bay area stood at minus-16 degrees, warming up only three degrees by the 1 p.m. kickoff. As it turned out, the record low temperature of minus-19 for December 31 occurred in the last hour of the year.

Meteorologist H.H. Bomalaski, in emphasizing the unexpected nature of the sudden freeze, said the average temperature for the month had actually been above the historical average.

Waking up on New Year's Eve, *Green Bay Press-Gazette* subscribers were able to read about a Chicago policeman being suspended when it was discovered that he was a grand dragon for the Ku Klux Klan in Illinois and had weapons, ammunition and KKK literature in his apartment.

They were also able to enjoy the sort of local sentiment that Bob Woessner's Sunday column breathed from Page Two of the *Press-Gazette*.

Vincent T. Lombardi is on record believing that three things are important to his men. Their religion, their families and the Green Bay Packers.

The statement is repeated not as a tribute but as a warning to the visitors in our midst. Take heed – this is no day to toy with the sensitivities of the populace.

The resident here is a man of great good humor – on all days except three. Those are, of course, the three days of the year which championship games are played. On any other day the jest about the sled races, mackinaws, the little butter and eggs from on the tundra and the rest of the clichés will be tolerated. They may even be smiled at.

But the man who slyly inquires today as to what they do with the sidewalks after 9 p.m. is likely to get a rap in the snout for his trouble. It will be wise, too, not to broadcast your loyalties if they do not happen to ride with the Green and Gold. Packer fans are allowed to voice quiet doubts and fears over the outcome of the impending game. Outsiders are not.

People from Green Bay do not go to Texas and make fun of the Alamo. Wise Texans and others will make no snide references about the shrine that is the Green Bay Packers. Derogatory comments about coaches, players, civic embellishments, bridges and local customs will certainly bring mutters – perhaps, violence.

The Packer fan in this, his hour of anxiety, must be given wide berth. Even wives and children will sense that they must step softly and speak low until the issue is settled. Because today, there is only one religion, there is only one family in this town.

Late in the afternoon, when another league pennant flies atop Lambeau Field then, perhaps, the visitor can make his little jest about snowshoes and such. He may still get belted for his effort – but it will be a much friendlier poke in the eye.

Fans bundle up in the sunshine on the visitor's side of Lambeau Field during the Ice Bowl. (Photo courtesy of the Green Bay Press-Gazette)

1 p.m. - Game Time

Paul Minten, the fifteen-year-old who had abandoned any thoughts of selling peanuts, had helped roll the tarp off the field. He was sequestered in the southeast corner of the field and had his first thrill before kickoff. Broadcasters Ray Scott and former Giants running back Frank Gifford walked past him as they surveyed the field before returning to the warmer press box.

Packers defensive back Herb Adderley (26) tackles Cowboys running back Dan Reeves as linebacker Dave Robinson (89) pursues during second-half action. Note the flags in the north end zone signalling a brisk northwest wind. (Photo courtesy of Joe Bowers)

Ron Fassbender, who had turned down the chance to sell his ticket to wealthy Dallas fans, found his seat in the south end zone. In front of him were several well-dressed couples, including a woman who didn't notice when Fassbender's brother spilled his hot chocolate on the back of her fur coat.

The brothers decided to go to the bathroom near the end of the first half, but the line getting in was too long. So they walked the short distance down Ridge Road to their parents' home, took care of matters, and then walked back into the stadium midway through the third quarter.

Bob Woessner wasn't going to complain about his assigned spot in the press box even though it didn't include a chair. But he found himself right in front of a space heater, and while thousands were coping with the bitter cold and other reporters were trying to wipe the fog off the press box windows with handkerchiefs and credit cards, Woessner was dealing with sweat running down his back.

Midshipman Bob VandeWalle found his seat – the single season ticket his dad had purchased when the new stadium opened in 1957 – and enjoyed watching the Packers take a 14-0 lead. He was also bolstered by a flask of brandy that his dad provided to help keep him warm. He shivered with everyone else throughout halftime, joining fellow fans in standing and stomping feet to keep the toes warm.

He needed a bathroom break, but discovered the men's room wasn't heated very well and the water had been turned off so the pipes wouldn't freeze. He watched the vapor clouds rise over the stadium in the second half, and sensed a pall among the fans who feared the Packers' dynasty might be coming to an end. But a couple first downs on a final fourth-quarter drive aroused him and the fans around him.

The first sale that Ken Vanderloop made to a beer buyer in the stands didn't work out. When he removed the cap, beer flowed out and immediately froze, forming an ice cream cone appearance. So Vanderloop took his case of beer to the men's restroom, where hordes of fans were gathered before the game started.

Within minutes, he sold every bottle of beer to fans who would pee and drink.

Vanderloop and his brother, Ed, took the empty cases and planted themselves on the stadium steps behind the Packers bench and watched the game.

Paul Casanova realized quickly that the tennis shoes he was wearing were not going to let his feet survive the cold. So, as the game began, he retreated to the men's restroom where there were many other comfort-seekers and some heat. Someone had a transistor radio, and Casanova stayed there until the game ended.

Bruce Mommaerts and the rest of the field crew huddled in a warm boiler room throughout the first half, then were summoned to the field at halftime. Their job was to sweep and shovel any ice or snow that had collected on the playing field. The steam they noticed when they first removed the tarp before the game had been replaced by crispy ice. The field was now rock hard.

Gene Lamers, an engineer from Combined Locks, south of Green Bay, watched the first half with his friend, Jerry Kamps, from their stadium seats. Kamps needed to warm up at halftime and walked back to their car for some heat. Lamers decided to find heat closer by. The teams were in their locker rooms, so Lamers hopped over the fence and took a seat near a heater on the Cowboys' bench. Undisturbed by anyone, he stayed there for the rest of the game, often sitting alongside Dallas quarterback Don Meredith.

Patti Kramer was grateful for the cardboard that her father cut up for her and her mother. But the game wasn't too far along when Patti realized she had too many socks on and her toes were freezing inside the tight boots. So she took the boots off and watched the rest of the game with her stocking feet inside the sleeping bag.

Roger Schneider, age ten, was planted in front of the television set in his Chilton home, thirty-five miles south of Green Bay. His grandfather watched the game with him and encouraged his grandson to calm down after he celebrated when the Packers took their 14-0 lead. It's a long game, he was told.

Kate Sorensen was finding her job at one of the Proski Concessions stands unproductive and cold. There were few customers, and she and her sister were just trying to stay warm. Finally, before the second quarter was very far along, word came that the concession stands were closing. The twins' father came to pick them up, first insisting to Proski that his daughters be paid. Kate Soresnen would see Bart Starr's winning quarterback sneak on TV the following day.

Bob Schulze, sports director for the Green Bay NBC television station, WFRV, was positioned in an open-air section of the press box where he was trying to thread film into his camera with bare hands. It was painful.

Brad and Ladd Nuss, the fence jumpers, and their friend, Dick Rifleman, developed a workable strategy to watch the game. They started at a south ramp, where they would watch a handful of plays before being told to move on by the usher. So they moved to the next ramp, and so forth around the stadium. Finally, midway through the third quarter, they noticed the crowd thinning out, so they walked to the top row of the stadium and gradually worked their way down.

Fifteen-year-old Dan Shalhoub, and his thirteen-year-old brother, Tony, had tickets, but they weren't sitting together. Dan and his friend, Dan Mercier, sat together and were uncomfortably cold. Even in the early part of the game, Dan Shalhoub was looking forward to when he could go home.

Joe Jarosh spent most of the game on his feet because it served two purposes. It helped him see the game because the people in front of him were often standing, and it also gave him a chance to stomp his feet to keep them warm.

Cal Lawton, the Peace Corps volunteer baking in the Argentina heat, listened to the start of the game from his hotel room in Buenos Aires. He took a cab to the airport and checked in, then went to the open air upper deck to get better radio reception. As the Packers began their final, game-winning drive, Lawton heard over the public address system, "Mr. Lawton, please come to the gate." His flight was ready for takeoff.

Tyler McCormack and Gary Wayne Cooper propped themselves atop an armored personnel carrier and listened to the game during their two-hour guard shift in Vietnam. They kept the volume low, for obvious reasons, and reported hourly to the Tactical Operations Center that there was no sign of enemy activity.

Rocky Bleier and his dad waited until right before kickoff to find their seats since Rocky had to make his way with crutches. Right away, he regretted even coming to the game.

Joe Bowers watched the first half of the game from his seat, but told his friend at halftime that he was going to see if he could get down to the field. Then he caught a break. After deciding he wouldn't be able to get past the five police officers at the north ramp to the field, he saw *Appleton Post-Crescent* sports editor John Paustian heading toward the field, apparently to check it out. Bowers had played football at Appleton High School and

Joe Bowers captured this image of the sheltered Packers' bench from his position on the sideline during the second half of the Ice Bowl. (Photo courtesy of Joe Bowers)

knew Paustian, so he fell in at Paustian's heels with his best staff photographer impersonation.

Anticipating that he would be halted by one of the security officers, Bowers sauntered right past them and found himself on the field. He went directly to a spot behind the Packers' bench and

Joe Bowers was close enough to snap this photo of Packers coach Vince Lombardi during the second half of the Ice Bowl. (Photo courtesy of Joe Bowers)

knelt to pretend he was adjusting his camera – an Instamatic – and waited for the teams to return to the field.

Bobbi Conard and her friend, Mary Ellen, found the line going into the women's bathroom too long, so they decided to slip behind the building and try to get in the back door. A security guard stopped them and told them the facility was for women only. The men's restroom was a short distance away. The women were wearing so many clothes that their gender was concealed.

Dick Egan kept himself warm enough with the chili and chicken soup he brought with him. He heard a woman sitting behind him tell her husband she was too cold and wanted to leave. Her husband handed her the car keys, and he stayed.

David Bunker, a twenty-year-old St. Norbert College student, didn't have tickets for the game, but he and his brother, Tom, decided to walk into the stadium when the gates opened at halftime. They found seats in the south end zone section, but soon realized they hadn't worn warm enough clothes, both in gym shoes. The Packers were behind, so the Bunker brothers debated whether to stay for the finish or head for a warm car.

Frank Steffel, the high school student with beer under his winter coat, had had no trouble getting his refreshment past the gate-keepers at the stadium. But he was finding out that the cold beer was getting too cold. He took several trips to the bathroom, eventually dumping the cans in the trash.

Jay Erbeck and Kathleen Berens, their wedding invitations set to be mailed, found their seats in the northeast corner of the stadium in what used to be called the kids section.

Pam Duebler and her school girlfriend had to seek refuge and warmth in the women's restroom, where they were joined by several women – apparently from Dallas – who were dressed in short skirts, nylons, and dressy gloves. No hats. The women were telling anyone who would listen that they had no intention of returning to their seats. When Pam and her friend did go back to their seats, they were quietly handed small bottles of brandy by

Pam's father, Chester, with the instruction that his body-warming gesture didn't need to be relayed to the girls' mothers.

Jim Buchholz, denied the job of setting up chairs at WLUK, still had a task. At halftime, he drove the two blocks to the stadium and stood in the parking lot below the press box. First half film was lowered to him, and he drove it to the airport where an ABC-TV jet was waiting to fly it to Chicago.

Jim Vandenberg, a Marquette University sophomore, was sitting on the wooden benches above the south end zone with his father. Not very comfortable, but fans were passing bottles down the row and the Vandenbergs warmed themselves with the passing Southern Comfort.

Steve Seidl and his father, Len, waited until halftime to light the charcoal they had crammed into the coffee can, preparing to use its heat to warm their toes. But the plan backfired. Apparently, the Seidls went overboard with the lighter fluid.

The flames shot straight up and were so hot that they virtually melted the back of the ski jacket of the man sitting in front of them. The smoke caused by the instant inferno did not go over well with fans nearby. Steve Seidl went to work quelling the blaze while his father worked out a settlement with the man whose jacket no longer existed in its original form.

JoAnn and Don Hanaway arrived at halftime, but JoAnn was suffering. Her toes were getting numb and she was second-guessing her decision to leave her injured two-year-old with a babysitter.

Joe Taycher was another of those teenagers who was paid to sell drinks in the stands. But the soda he was trying to peddle

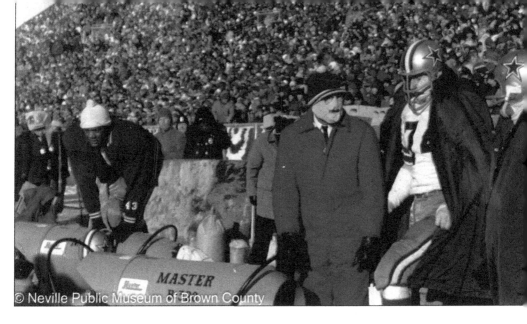

Dallas Cowboys players and staff attempt to grab some heat from the blowers operating on their sideline. (Photo courtesy of the Neville Public Museum of Brown County)

froze, and there were few buyers of the coffee and hot chocolate. So he found a place to sit and joined the ranks of fan in the stands.

Rod Kowalczyk, De Pere High School teacher and basketball coach, used his dad's tickets in section 22, row 24 to watch the game with Don Kollath, the best man at his wedding. Joining them for the game were ample supplies of hot chocolate and peppermint schnapps.

Mark Thompson had his seat in the north end zone stands thanks to his Uncle Guy's invitation and the state trooper's delivery. But by halftime, Guy had had enough and headed home. Many other fans did the same, so Mark gradually worked his way down to the second row to watch the rest of the game.

Ray Barrington, the ten-year-old from Hortonville, couldn't feel his feet by halftime, so his mother decided to get him home.

They sat in the car for twenty minutes while it warmed up, then drove toward home through Oneida, Seymour, and Black Creek.

Ted Jones, who received his tickets from Packers running back Chuck Mercein's wife, was so cold early in the third quarter that he retreated to the fire department warming trailer outside the north end zone tunnel. He returned to his seat just in time to see Dallas score a go-ahead touchdown on the first play of the fourth quarter.

Tom Hinz, the city police officer stationed at one of the stadium ramps, used halftime to escape to the NFL Films Greyhound bus to get warm. He heard complaints from NFL Films employees about their film breaking because of the cold.

Rob Van Gemert and his brother made a feeble attempt to ski at Pine Mountain in Iron Mountain, Michigan, but were driven inside by the cold. Awaiting them there was a seat in front of a warm fireplace and a television set showing the Packers-Cowboys game. A win-win.

Susan Creviere's solitude at Our Lady of Charity convent was soon interrupted by the sounds of nuns cheering as they gathered around a radio. Noise from the stadium, less than two miles to the east, also invaded the convent walls.

Keith Budzis wasn't going to wait until the end of the game to find out if the acetylene torches were going to come in handy. As the fourth quarter was beginning, he and Bill Boyea went to Budzis's car and brought the equipment back into the stadium. They wheeled the carts down a ramp to the field, knowing they wouldn't be challenged because of the lax security and the fact they would appear to be part of a work crew. They approached a Civil Defense official and asked him to watch the torches. The man called a superior who told him to do exactly that.

Budzis and Boyea then walked down close to the Packers bench and watched the exciting finish to the game.

Tom Ebert, a ten-year-old living in the village of Allouez, sat with his father, Fred. But there were frequent trips to the bathroom, where father would prop son up on a sink and rub his feet to help regain circulation.

Prior to halftime, Peter Helf and David Martin delivered sandwiches to the game officials' locker room. Beer would be delivered after the game. Helf and Martin spent part of the game in a concession storeroom and part inside the press box.

Chapter 9

Green Bay in 1967

Green Bay, without the Packers, would have had nothing to apologize for in 1967. It boasted a foundation of community spirit that was strengthened by its willingness to change and grow. Its reputation in pro football circles was solidly embedded in the "small city with a great team tradition" image. But it wasn't lacking for credits that helped attract people and commerce. Business leadership was one of its staples.

Its population increased 167 percent from 1920 until the day of the Ice Bowl, topping out at 82,788. The ethnic heritage was German, Belgian, Polish, and Irish – all impacted in some way by the nearby Native American culture in Oneida.

Alice in Dairyland for 1966 Joann Cuprey poses with a large bulk of cheese made for Borden Foods as part of a promotional campaign for the State of Wisconsin. (Photo courtesy of the Neville Public Museum of Brown County)

The city had thirty-five parks and sixty-two churches representing eighteen denominations. It was served by four railroads, five fire stations with 128 firemen, and a police force that included 116 men and one policewoman.

Its business anchors were the four large paper mills, three pulp mills, and four paper converting companies. Its harbor boasted the movement of 2.5 million tons of goods in 1967, including coal, stone, wood, pulp, steel, sulphur, grain, petroleum products, and sugar.

Green Bay was the country's largest cheese processing and shipping center.

There was one daily newspaper, three radio stations, three television stations, two hotels and twenty-one motels in the city.

Four railroads served the city, and there were eighteen terminals for twenty-four truck lines.

In the year leading up to the Ice Bowl, major change took place both downtown and on the city's fringe. An urban renewal project called Gregby 1 was approved, promising the downtown development of a pedestrian mall. The city was also set to profit by North Central Airlines' announcement that it instituted DC-9 jet service to Austin Straubel Airport, a move that increased boardings 19 percent over 1966.

A major step was taken to consolidate adjacent Brown County communities into a single library system, with the prospect of eventually building a new library in downtown Green Bay to replace the aged Kellogg Library on South Jefferson Street.

A comprehensive study completed two months before the Ice Bowl recommended that three major bridges be constructed before 1985 to advance the city and county's role as a regional transportation hub. The priorities were a bridge to connect the villages of Ashwaubenon and Allouez, one to span the convergence of the Fox River and the bay of Green Bay at Tower Drive, and one south of De Pere. (As of this writing, the bridge south of De Pere was still in the discussion stage, some fifty-five years later.)

The Brown County Historical Society went on record to request that property north of the reformatory in Allouez be used for a historical mall or state park (today's Heritage Hill State

Park). The American Automobile Association honored Green Bay as one of twelve state cities for outstanding pedestrian safety. The Wisconsin Wildlife Federation said the Brown County Conservation Alliance was the most outstanding conservation group in 1967. But the US Bureau of Labor Statistics listed Green Bay as the twenty-sixth most expensive city to live in because of high housing costs.

But nothing was more significant for the Green Bay community's future than the establishment of a four-year university campus as part of the University of Wisconsin system. Under the guidance of newly hired Chancellor Ed Weidner, the university was being developed with an emphasis on the environment.

University of Wisconsin-Green Bay chancellor Edward Weidner (right) leads a site tour of the Shorewood property to early campus administrators (from left) Robert Maier, Raymond Vlasin, and Keith White in September 1967. (Photo courtesy of University of Wisconsin-Green Bay Archives)

Ground breaking had taken place several months before the Ice Bowl, although there were still legal attempts from communities to the south of Green Bay opposing the location.

The site – on a portion of Shorewood Golf Course on the city's northeast side – gained full approval by the UW Board of Regents in 1967, although Brown County had to start condemnation proceedings when it couldn't reach a purchase agreement with the golf course ownership. While this was going on, Assemblyman William Rogers of Kaukauna introduced a bill to have the site moved to the Larsen Farms site on Green Bay's west side. His bill passed the Assembly, but was voted down in the Senate.

The four-year university with more than 2,000 students was on schedule to open in 1970.

Regionally, one of the most impactful events of 1967 was the initial construction of a nuclear generation plant in nearby Kewaunee County by Wisconsin Public Service and two other power companies. The $80 million operation was scheduled to be completed by 1972.

Chapter 10

4 p.m. - Celebration

The Drive

First down at the Green Bay 32-yard line: Starr swing pass to Anderson gains 6 yards

Second down at the Green Bay 38: Mercein gains 7 around right end

First down at the Green Bay 45: Starr pass to Dowler for 13 yards

First down at the Dallas 42: Anderson tackled for 9-yard loss by Townes

Second down at the Green Bay 49: Starr swing pass to Anderson gains 12

Third down at the Dallas 39: Starr swing pass to Anderson gains 9

First down at the Dallas 30: Starr pass to Mercein gains 19

First down at the Dallas 11: Mercein gains 8 over left tackle

Second down at the Dallas 3: Anderson gains 2 over right guard

First down at the Dallas 1: Anderson stopped for no gain

Second down at the Dallas 1: Anderson stopped for no gain

Third down at the Dallas 1: Starr scores touchdown on quarterback sneak

Mercein's 19-yard gain was the last play that Rocky Bleier and his father would see. Knowing there would be difficulty maneuvering through the crowd after the game ended, they decided to leave early. As they reached their car, they heard the roar of the crowd that signaled Starr's winning touchdown. Rocky Bleier would see the play later on the TV highlights.

Harlan and Fred Ihlenfeldt stayed until the end and, when it was over, they decided to show off the bedsheet they brought to the game. Fred stood up and waved the huge sign that read: "TEXAS HAS THE LONE STAR BUT WE HAVE THE BRIGHT STARR. 1967 CHAMPS."

Joe Weiss, the sixteen-year-old doing a play-by-play into his tape recorder, hollered, "I don't believe it!" His uncle, Dave, sitting next to him and providing fictitious color commentary, yelled "Bart!" Joe's dad, Bill, just said he was too frozen to yell.

Running back Chuck Mercein (30) and guard Jerry Kramer (64) are all smiles as they come off the field following the play that gave the Packers the lead in the Ice Bowl. (Photo courtesy of Joe Bowers)

David and Tom Bunker couldn't foresee the dramatic finish to the Ice Bowl. But they knew, sitting in their south end zone seats, that their near-frozen feet needed a warm car, and immediately. So, with minutes still showing on the scoreboard clock, the brothers trudged to the parking lot. As they reached the car, they heard the roar of the Lambeau Field crowd. Turning on the car radio, they learned that Starr not only scored a winning touchdown, but that he did it immediately below where the Bunkers had been sitting.

Bob VandeWalle was caught up in the screaming and hugging after Starr's sneak, then waited out the suspense of the final two Cowboys desperation passes. He wanted to rush the field, but his father said his mother was freezing and they needed to return to their parked 1961 blue Chevy. It was on the drive home that they passed a burning house in the village of Ashwaubenon, with the sight of frozen ice draped around the structure.

Reporter Bob Woessner navigated the sixty steps down to the field, then weaved through the celebrators to the entrance to the Packers' locker room. It was warm inside, and Woessner watched Lombardi hug players and coaches. Interviews and observations

Packers quarterback Bart Starr confers with Coach Vince Lombardi late in the Ice Bowl. Joe Bowers snapped this photo from his position along the Packers' sideline. (Photo courtesy of Joe Bowers)

gave him what he needed for his story but, with the *Press-Gazette* not publishing the following day, he just went home.

Cal Lawton, the Peace Corps worker, made his flight from Buenos Aires to Santiago, although the takeoff was delayed for ten minutes because he didn't report to the gate until the Packers had won. He received a few nasty looks from other passengers and was glad he didn't tell them why he was tardy.

Young Charlie Yeager spent the entire game at the WLUK-TV studios where his father, Bob, worked. The station is just two blocks from Lambeau Field, and when Starr scored the touchdown, Charlie and his cousin ran outside to listen to the roar of the crowd. However, the door slammed and locked them outside. Everyone inside was busy cheering, and the two boys spent about fifteen minutes in the frigid air before someone opened the door.

Joe Bowers wasn't going to move. He knelt behind the Packers' bench with other photographers and began taking pictures. He knew he had a good one of Starr conferring with Lombardi late in the game. While the post-game pandemonium continued on the field, Bowers put his camera away, picked up one of the small benches the Packers had been using, put it over his back, walked out of the stadium, and loaded it into his hatchback car in the parking lot.

Gene Lamers, the thirty-one-year-old papermaker from Combined Locks, was still sitting on the Cowboys' bench when Starr scored. When a Dallas coach yelled "Offense!" and Meredith got up to get ready for his last-second desperation passes, his warmup cape fell at Lamers's feet. Quickly, the man who had no business being there picked up the cape, rolled it up into a ball, and stuffed it under his coat. When the Cowboys were walking deject-

Gene Lamers displays the warmup cape worn by Cowboys quarterback Don Meredith that he pilfered out of Lambeau Field. (Photo courtesy of Paul Vidani)

edly back to their locker room, Lamers was walking out of Lambeau Field with a souvenir he would show off at the numerous bars he visited on his way home.

The Eggerts, of Oshkosh, who chose football over church and traded their midfield tickets for ones in the end zone, were rewarded because they sat in the tenth row immediately in front of where Starr scored.

Jim Buchholz was back at the stadium, this time waiting for film from the second half to be dropped down from the press box.

Back he went to the airport to hand it off to the ABC network official, and this time was rewarded with two $50 bills for his effort. Not bad, he thought, for someone making $1.85 an hour.

Brad and Ladd Nuss, the gate crashers, went down on the field, and Ladd helped take down the north goalpost. Then they returned to Dick Rifleman's Volkswagen and warmth.

Richard Baldwin asked his dad if he could go to the field when the game ended and got the OK, although Bob Baldwin said he'd pass on that experience and meet him at their warmed-up car. Richard reached the field in time to pat a couple Packers players on the back and saw someone grab Lombardi's hat. He then made his way for one of the wooded Packers helmet displays attached to the base of the stands. He managed to rip off a part of one before a police officer told him that was enough. Richard had his memory and his souvenir.

Frank Steffel was also part of a goalpost demolition crew and even hung on the pole for a while. He considered helping lug the goalpost downtown, but decided instead that post-game recovery at a packed Candlestick Bar downtown made more sense.

Jim Vandenberg headed to the parking lot and saw many fans trying to locate their cars. Nobody could remember where they parked. Did you see a red Camaro? Did you see a blue Mustang?

Leland Baenen, a dairy farmer, was part of the Brown County Sheriff's Auxiliary Police and was stationed in a stairwell on the southern end of the field. Moments before Starr's winning sneak at the other end of the stadium, Beanen was told by Joe Nockerts, his supervisor, to get down on the field by the goalposts.

After Starr's touchdown, stadium manager Wally Proski told

Baenen to remove the padding from the goalposts before fans stormed the field. Down on the field, Baenen told one of the officials about his assignment and was told to wait until the final play was over. When the last incompletion confirmed the Packers' victory, Beanen and a co-worker removed the padding, then rushed it to a first-aid room under the stadium.

Baenen hurried back to the field, where he was part of the cordon that escorted Lombardi to the locker room.

Larry Pierquet was an usher, but when the game ended he joined the throngs on the field. He climbed the south goalpost and helped to pull it down. He then joined others in dragging part of it out of the stadium to a house three blocks away, where it was cut into pieces.

Michael Lefebvre didn't sell any beer, but he had hung around for the game and happily stormed the field at the end. He was rewarded with a piece of the goalpost that he helped take down, and watched as it was cut into shares nearby.

Peter Helf's all-access pass allowed him to go down to the field for the exciting finish of the game. He took his turn hanging on a goalpost after the game, then grabbed one of the wooden helmet decorations that adorned the stadium and took it home.

Mark Thompson wasn't going to miss the fun on the field or the chance to find a souvenir. He jumped the fence at the final gun and spotted flags at the corners of the end zone. But a member of the grounds crew quickly picked them up. So Thompson instead scoured the area of the Packers' bench and saw some white towels with green stripes. He grabbed one, then headed for his uncle's house, and eventually took a Greyhound back to Oshkosh.

Glen (Bucky) Hansen (right) was a member of the Lambeau Field grounds crew for thirty years, including for the Ice Bowl. He took home one of the wooden Packers helmets that decorated the stadium. (Photo courtesy of Laura Laurent)

Perhaps no one had a better view of Starr's touchdown than Paul Minten, sitting on the southeast corner of the field. Minten started to rush the field to congratulate Starr, but found himself face-to-face with a Cowboys lineman who was walking off the field. Minten went back to his seat, where he watched the final plays as the frustrated Cowboys yelled for a pass interference call that never came. One of the Dallas players flung his helmet that landed about fifteen feet from Minten. Tempted to pick it up, Minten didn't.

Steve Kerkes might have wanted to join the on-field revelry, but he had to get back to the Oneida Country Club and his job as a busboy. He was rewarded when Lombardi made an appearance and even handed out $20 bills to the Oneida staff.

Susan Creviere knew that something big had happened as she heard the roar from the stadium reach her convent two miles away. And the nuns in a nearby room were cheering.

Officer Tom Hinz was freed from his post at the stadium, but had to go directly to the intersection of Ridge Road and Ninth Street north of the stadium to direct traffic.

Ray Barrington and his mother continued to listen to the game as they drove toward their Hortonville home. When the Packers drove close to the goal line, Ray's mother pulled over in front of a bank in Shiocton, where they heard Starr's sneak.

Bob Murphy and Bob Kaminski, two friends from Two Rivers, joined the throng on the field when the game ended. They had no interest in helping with the goalpost removal, but spotted a bench on the Packers' sideline. They picked it up and carried it to their car before finding a place to warm up with some drinks.

Jim and Janis Blean stayed until the end of the game, but when they prepared to leave, they realized that the rubber hot water bottle they had put at the bottom of their sleeping bag had sprung a leak. The water froze immediately and all but welded the sleeping bag to the concrete below. Several tugs freed it.

Ten-year-old Tom Ebert was relieved that the game was over. He had spent portions of the afternoon in the stadium men's room where his father, Fred, sat him on a sink and rubbed his feet to warm them up. They headed for their car in the northeast corner of the parking lot and found a group of men crowded around a large piece of the goalpost that they had dragged from the stadium.

Tom Ebert poses with a section of an Ice Bowl goalpost and an autographed print of the winning play. (Photo courtesy of Paul Vidani)

Fred Ebert, a machinist at Nelson Machinery on Pearl Street downtown, negotiated a deal with the men. If they would help him load the goalpost into the back of his car, he would call his boss to get the shop opened.

So the Eberts, with young Tom thawing out in the passenger seat next to a large and cold piece of aluminum – and several strangers loaded in the back seat – drove to the shop. Fred Ebert cut the goalpost into pieces and Ice Bowl souvenirs were born.

It was a little more complicated for Keith Budzis and Bill Boyea. They joined the throngs of people on the field when the game ended, and Boyea took a turn hanging on the north goalpost as it was being wrenched from its foundation.

When it was finally snapped free, Budzis told his collaborators that he could take it to a garage and cut it into pieces. So, with the help of others, they hauled the goalposts out of the stadium. Budzis put the top down on his convertible – and heard the car window glass

Keith Budzis still has this large piece of the north goalpost he helped cut up following the Ice Bowl. (Photo courtesy of Keith Budzis)

shatter in the process – and the goalpost was loaded on the open car. They drove down Highland Avenue (today's Lombardi Avenue) with a caravan of would-be souvenir seekers following, and reached the garage on Main Street.

There, Budzis and Boyea used a power band saw to cut the post into pieces, handing them out to the others while the supply lasted. Budzis kept a large piece for himself, then he and Boyea drove to downtown Green Bay to show it off to hundreds of people celebrating the Packers' victory.

Ken and Ed Vanderloop, who watched the finish of the game as they sat on their empty beer cases, joined the throng on the field and helped cut up the fallen goalposts. They eventually acquired a piece and wrote their names on it with clear black marker. Ken Vanderloop planned to show it off at Whipp's Goalpost bar, where he worked as a bartender. First, the brothers cut off a thin piece of the goalposts for themselves.

Pam Duebler and her father, Chester, watched the post-game celebration that included the dismantling of the goalposts. What they would find out two days later was that one of Chester's workers at Mirro Aluminum was part of the on-field melee. He obtained a piece of goalpost and would give it to Chester when he returned to work.

The UW-La Crosse band was loaded into warm buses, driven to Oshkosh for dinner, then taken home.

Bruce Mommaerts watched the pandemonium on the field, then began cleaning up the empty stands, collecting mittens or scarves that had been left there and picking up empty bottles and trash. He then prepared for his normal post-game job of cleaning the bathrooms, but was told by a supervisor that he wouldn't be permitted to clean the women's bathroom this time.

Apparently, he was told, there were a couple underdressed and over-intoxicated women who had passed out in there. Not the place for a fifteen-year-old boy.

Paul (P.J.) Vidani holds a piece of goalpost from the Ice Bowl in his never-ending quest to document stories from the game. (Photo courtesy of Paul Vidani).

Chapter 11

Ice Bowl Obsession

Paul (P.J.) Vidani's path to obsession wasn't the standard route. Little in his past explains why he decided to go to such extremes to uncover stories about the Ice Bowl, a game whose importance at the time took second fiddle to the history term paper he had to complete that day at St. Thomas College.

Vidani had a geographical connection to the Packers of that era, having spent his high school years at the family home on Sunset Drive in Allouez, close enough to the Lombardi home that he was included in an occasional wine drinking episode with the coach's daughter, Susan.

Any budding interest in the events of December 31, 1967, remained dormant for more than thirty years as Vidani charted a career path that included ownership of Green Bay Blueprint beginning in 1976. Questions about the Ice Bowl began dancing in his head around 1998, eventually prompting him to go to extremes to find the answers.

What did people do at the Ice Bowl? Why did they go to the game? Which Ice Bowl stories are true and which ones are fabricated? And what was the common denominator in a story that pitted good versus evil – Packers fans versus the bitter cold?

So Vidani went to the site of that confrontation to get some answers, setting up a makeshift stand outside Lambeau Field on the days of Packers games with a sign that read, "Were You at the Ice Bowl?"

Fans with Ice Bowl stories to share stopped to talk, and Vidani recorded their comments on his video camera. Some stories were entertaining. Some were fascinating. Some were typical. And some, he realized, were phony.

"I knew some were bullshitting me," he said. "But a lot of people wanted to talk about it, to get their memories off their chest."

He did it because .... well, we'll let him explain it.

***

I went to the playoff game at Lambeau Field in 1998. My buddy, Dan, brought two metal hacksaws that we displayed while sitting in our seats. We were having fun "threatening" to cut down the goalposts after the game, and prompting wild cheers of those around us. Security officials got worried and confiscated the hacksaws by the second quarter. Everybody laughed at the prank and we won the game. But I then realized that a lot of fans, especially the young ones, knew very little about the Ice Bowl, when the goal post removal became famous. I also realized that most of the Ice Bowl attendees soon would be dead and their stories of that day would never be told.

I knew that the Ice Bowl was a historical event not only for the Green Bay Packers players, but also for the frozen fans sitting in the stands. What other sporting event commanded such attention? What was the origin of the newly created phrase "The Frozen Tundra?" What did this event say about these fans who endured three hours and fifteen minutes of pain? And what provoked them to stay longer and storm the field in such cold for another thirty minutes or so? Did the fans actually start charcoal fires with in Folgers coffee tins? Did the sleeping bags work? Did anybody get frostbite or even die? And whatever happened to the mysterious woman from Dallas who came dressed in a miniskirt? Even my father, who had been on an Antarctic expedition for six months in 1946-47, commented to me, "It was as cold as the #*&#@$ Antarctic that day."

Many of these Ice Bowl stories seemed suspicious to me. Myths. Local folklore without any verification. Stories that originated in bars and taverns while drinking beer and Old Fashions. And yet they were gaining credibility over time. And these people in these fables were dying and their stories would be lost forever.

I determined that there were two groups who endured the cold the best: farmers and deer hunters. So, who were the others whose occupations and lifestyles did not prepare them for this day?

The answers could not be found on the newly created internet. So I decided to track these people down, video camera in hand, and ask them myself. I needed empirical evidence. The *Green Bay Press-Gazette* picked up my story and put it in the newspaper. From that time forward, the word spread and people who were there (or their fathers, grandmothers, uncles, and aunts) started to call me and/or send me or email their stories between 2004 and 2006.

Paul (P.J.) Vidani hands out these cards in his efforts to collect stories about his favorite subject, the Ice Bowl.

Starting in 2004, I went filming with Leland Baenen, a farmer from Casco, who was a security officer at the Ice Bowl. I walked around Lambeau Field calling out for Ice Bowl "survivors" to tell me their stories. I had a megaphone in one hand and my small Canon 600 camera in the other. I interviewed over 200 people, truth-tellers and fibbers alike.

To verify their truthfulness, I asked these people if they had any souvenirs from the game such as ticket stubs, game day magazines, etc. People began bringing me tangible items proving that they were there (or other family members who were there, but had passed on). These included photos sent to me of these souvenirs that included the following:

- More than twenty chunks of the two goalposts torn down that day (each valued at $400 plus). The sizes varied from two inches wide to five feet long.

- An actual Dallas Cowboys warmup cape stolen by a Packers fan at the last minute of the game. Don Meredith's son certified the authenticity of the cape in a 2017 documentary of the game.

- Game Day magazines (currently valued at over $400).

- Ticket stubs from the game (each valued at $500 plus). One guy had two complete tickets, not torn. He admitted he stayed home and did not use the tickets at all.

- A bench stolen from Lambeau Field after the game.

- Two wooden Packers helmets (5 feet x 4 feet). One later was appraised on the TV show *Antique Road Show* in 2019 for $3,000 plus.

- An 8mm homemade movie, nine minutes long, of the game.

- A stadium usher at the game gave me his actual usher ID button along with a photo of him at the game climbing up a goalpost that he helped tear down.

- Various instructional signage ripped off and taken home to be forever displayed and identified (as to its origins) in fans' basements honoring Packers legacy and the game itself, along with photos of Lombardi.

I fact-checked all these stories (some included narratives and souvenir relics passed onto them by their relatives) as having a high probability of being truthful.

Several people had suspicious stories that I discarded. One guy brought me an iconic crowd scene photo from the game and claimed that he was in the photo. But it turned out to be a false story. Another guy who had a terrific story about a ticket stub he had signed by Lombardi (a true story, it turned out), but demanded money for his story. He got no money. Nor did anybody else I interviewed.

Overall, most of the people I interviewed were truthful. To be on the safe side, I included only those stories that could be verified with solid evidence. Realizing soon that I lacked the skills to make a professional film, I decided instead to provide these taped interviews to the Packers. What was important to me then was to interview these attendees before they died. Some of these interviews were uploaded to YouTube and are still there. The entire Ice Bowl documentary film went dormant until 2021, when I was contacted by Tony Walter.

Very few small towns have great historical events. The Alamo, Little Big Horn, Gettysburg, Waterloo, and Bunker Hill hosted sad, bloody battles. Other significant sporting events tell little about their fans who sat in comfortable seats eating hot dogs and popcorn.

But the Ice Bowl was different. There was little hot food, and most of the beer and wine snuck into the game was soon frozen. The only places to warm up were the bathrooms, and they were filled to claustrophobic capacity during the entire game. The Packers had giant blowing heaters on the field. The fans could only build fires in small cans.

This wasn't the first sub-zero game in which these fans had cheered on their Packers, and it would not be the last. So what makes the game significant or even historical?

To be historical an event must:

Endure time – The game is mentioned every year by TV announcers for home games, especially in November-January. It is considered one of the best NFL games ever played. It not only endures, it grows in stature by the year. A small cottage industry pumps out hundreds of Ice Bowl merchandise items each year that include clothing, hats, pins, wine, carryon bags, books, videos, framed photos, 3D replicas of the stadium, bobble heads of Lombardi at the game, and even a pillow brandishing a large graphic ticket stub from the game.

Be unique – No other NFC game was played outside in minus 13-degree weather. It resulted in the fans there being united in a kind of symbiotic attachment to the Packers team that brought them that victory. That special relationship remains to this day.

Have an impact on people – The game resulted in the moniker "Frozen Tundra" being attached to Lambeau Field – and to the entire city itself. The name "Ice Bowl" is branded and seared into the memory of all football fans.

Be truthful – The events I reported on were not hearsay. I videotaped over 200 people, got their names, and even addresses and stories in their own words. Only those who had some kind of tangible proof (ticket stubs, goalpost parts, etc.) made the cut. Although not a perfect method for getting accuracy and authenticity, it filtered out a lot of false reporting.

I believe that the Ice Bowl of December 31, 1967, meets all these criteria. I am still looking for more Ice Bowl stories. A website will be set up for people to submit their stories and photos.

A local restaurant, The Union Hotel in De Pere, created a cocktail at my request appropriately named "The Ice Bowl Sneak" made with brandy, vodka and something else. It's served with a scoop of shaved ice and a yellow goalpost straw.

Chapter 12

New Year's Eve and --

Bob VandeWalle spent New Year's Eve at the De Pere Sportsman's Club with friends. They put their car keys on a table, and every hour one of them would go to the parking lot and start the vehicles.

Pete Sabel and Tim McDonough went to Smitty's Bar on Broadway in Green Bay after the game. Pete then took Kathleen Berensen to a New Year's Eve party that went far into the wee hours. He got home at 2:30 a.m., was awaken by his mother at 6 a.m. to go to church, then caught an 8 a.m. Greyhound to return to Army basic training in Kentucky. It was a trip that involved a lot of sleeping.

(From left) Bob Vande Walle, Ken Brosig, and Tom Bonfigt toast the Packers' Ice Bowl victory at the De Pere Sportsman's Club on a joyous New Year's Eve. (Photo courtesy of Bob VandeWalle)

Rod Kowalczyk found his way to Paul's Bar in downtown De Pere, where they saw a Dallas warmup jacket that had been confiscated by a fan. Kowalczyk and his wife, Bev, then hosted a New Year's Eve party at their home.

Many other fans gathered at Paul's Bar after the game. Someone brought in the ladder that belonged to the UW-La Crosse band that was supposed to perform at halftime, but didn't because of the bitter cold. Someone brought in a couple footballs and one even brought a Cowboys cape that supposedly belonged to receiver Bob Hayes.

The Weiss family wasn't finished with its Ice Bowl Day memory making. Dave Weiss had served on the Governor's Commission for Physical Fitness with Bart Starr, and he knew where the Starrs lived. So, sometime after warming up, he directed his family over to Chateau Drive, northwest of the stadium, and knocked on the door. Starr and his wife, Cherry, were on their way out to dinner with backup quarterback Zeke Bratkowski and his wife, but took a moment to greet the Weiss family.

Joe Jarosh went home to watch the game highlights on TV and decided he enjoyed that more than seeing the original, because he was warm.

Dan Shalhoub was happy to be in a warm place at home. He had noticed that his friend, Dan Mercier, had turned purple near the end of the game. Back at the Shalhoub home, the decision was made to put Dan in a hot tub of water to get his body temperature back to normal.

Several days after the Ice Bowl, Ken Vanderloop brought the goalpost piece to his job at Whipp's Goalpost Bar on Manitowoc

Dave Weiss (right) visits with Packers quarterback Bart Starr (center) and Ade Olson during the Region 6 Jogathon event a few months prior to the Ice Bowl. (Photo courtesy of Dave Weiss)

Road outside Green Bay. There, it was put on a shelf for customers to see. Vanderloop decided he would leave it there for a while before taking it home.

But when he returned to work the following week, he was stunned to find out that owner Eddie Whipp had sold the goalpost piece for $375. The goalpost piece, with the Vanderloop brothers' names written across it, was gone.

Chapter 13

Weather-Beaten Reactions

Ron Kramer, the former Packers tight end who was on the 1961 and 1962 championship teams, but now played for the Detroit Lions, said he knew how the game would end.

"I knew Bart Starr was going to carry the ball in for the touchdown," Kramer told the *Detroit Free Press*. "He had to. When you play for Vince Lombardi, you get the job done."

Ron Kramer

Many reactions centered on the weather, and some high-ranking football executives spoke of a weather solution that was never going to be enacted.

Tex Schramm, the general manager and architect of the Dallas Cowboys, certainly couldn't be blamed for his reaction to the Ice Bowl playing conditions. After all, most knowledgeable football observers concluded the Cowboys were the better team on December 31, 1967, but were struck down by the winter fates.

Schramm watched it all and then had a warm chair to watch the New Year's Day bowl games. That was enough to prompt his comment two days after the Ice Bowl.

"When I saw the four bowl games yesterday ... it was sickening to me that the greatest game of all couldn't have been played under the same circumstances. This leaves everybody wondering whether the best team is representing the NFL in the Super Bowl. The fault lies in that this is one of the last vestiges of the past in which the league has not kept up with the times.

"Now, with television and rapid transportation, to play a game as important as this one, in conditions not satisfactory for the game of football, is unfair to the players, the coaches and the fans of both teams because it does not determine which is the better football team."

Green Bay Press-Gazette sports editor Len Wagner chided Schramm in print, pointing out that the Cowboys only had themselves to blame for not holding on to the lead at the end. And he said playing the game in Green Bay was the right call.

"When I saw 50,000 people that turned out in that pneumonia-tempting weather," Wagner wrote three days after the game,

"I decided that the only ridiculous thing would be to take the game away from these great, loyal and avid fans who wanted to see their team win the championship in their town."

Former Packer Jim Temp, in his weekly column for his home-town newspaper, the *La Crosse Tribune*, wrote that the Cowboys had little basis for blaming the weather.

"As far as I'm concerned, that's a lot of Texas hot air," Temp wrote. "The Dallas Cowboys don't have a legitimate squawk. They were beaten, not by the weather, as they would like to have you believe, but because they failed to stand up under the intense pressure that the Packers seemed to thrive on.

"Sure, the Cowboys came from the relatively balmy climate of Dallas to Green Bay icebox and the attic air supposedly affected them more than the Packers. But nobody is immune to the sort of cold that this game was played in. Nobody gets used to that kind of weather.

"When the pressure descended with a thump in the final four minutes and the Packers, as is their delightful custom, began charging toward the goal, the Cowboys faltered. All of a sudden, the weather was too cold for them."

Schramm did find some immediate sympathizers, however.

Cleveland Browns owner Art Modell said the issue of a neutral, warm-weather site for championship games "will be discussed in no uncertain terms at our February meeting. I personally believe it should be moved to a neutral warm weather spot."

Modell, perhaps still smarting from the Browns' champion-ship game loss to the Packers in snowy Lambeau Field in 1965, said he would propose a two-year test of the neutral site plan.

Commissioner Pete Rozelle jumped onboard with the plan.

"I'm for it," Rozelle said. "I'll work to get it moved. Under the conditions it was played last Sunday, the game is unfair to both teams."

But Chicago Bears head coach and owner George Halas was having none of it.

"It's always been my contention that the fans who support a team through the season have a right to see the title game," Halas said. "The cold didn't seem to bother the great fans in Green Bay Sunday. I don't think they even felt the cold."

Halas said if any change in the policy is considered, it should still give the qualifying home team the option of either playing at home or going to a neutral site.

Published minutes from the NFL owners meeting in February 1968 include no reference to any motion or discussion about neutral sites.

Bill Van Vleet, who covered the game for the *Fort Worth Star-Telegram*, didn't take the side of the Cowboys when he addressed the neutral site issue.

"The harsh cold raised once again the question of whether the NFL should agree on a neutral city for its title game," he wrote two days after the game. "On the other hand, the Green Bay fans, with their weird costumes, were maybe having more fun than I was. And the home fans should be the first consideration of the league."

Bob Johnson, sports editor of the *Spokane Chronicle*, was impressed by the Packers fans.

"They say that America has become a nation of softies," Johnson wrote two days after the Ice Bowl "Well, those 50,000 who showed up in 14-below-zero weather to watch the title tilt may have been soft in the head, but they certainly belied the contention that Americans can't take it. It wasn't hard to understand why the players showed up. After all, they were playing for lots of loot. But the customers had to pay for the privilege of watching and freezing to death at the same time. It was something like making a condemned man pay for the electricity before the execution."

Green Bay native Red Smith, of the *New York Times*, wrote: "If Jethro Pugh was stomping through Kramer's dreams all last week, Pugh and his violent accomplices in the Dallas defensive line will be haunting Bart Starr for weeks to come, but Bart will be having his nightmares under a Miami moon. Starr bought the Packers tickets to the site of the Jan. 14 Stupor Bowl Sunday with a one-yard plunge that snatched the championship of the National Football League from the Cowboys' frozen fingers just 13 seconds before the end of the 35th annual title game."

Shirley Povich of the *Washington Post* wrote: "The Cowboys won the toss and there was some hope they would elect to call the whole thing off, but they didn't ... It was apparent that only on the Dallas side of the field was the temperature below zero."

Wrote Sam Blair of the *Dallas Morning News*: "When two penguins sauntered into the hotel drug store and bought hot water bottles, when waitresses ice-skated across the coffee shop to serve breakfast, when Admiral Byrd fetched out bags and carried them to the taxi, it really became obvious. All of us – the Cowboys, the Packers, the fans, the press – were trapped in a situation which the sports world had never experienced before. .... This was No Man's weather. .... No sporting event, with the possible exception of the Winter Olympics, ever had been contested in such brutal coldness."

Green Bay officials were counting the cost of the Ice Bowl. Clarence Nier, chairman of the Stadium Commission, said the goalposts were an estimated $2,000 loss.

Bill Brault, of the Green Bay Area Visitors and Convention Bureau, said approximately $2,100 worth of flags and banners were taken away from the stadium after the game.

Both men said the financial losses were worth it.

Epilogue

Jay Erbeck's leave from the Glenview Naval Air Station was long enough to allow him to watch the Packers' victory over Oakland in Super Bowl II with his fiancée, Kathleen Berens, in Green Bay. The following morning, he mailed their wedding invitations in downtown Green Bay, then headed back to Glenview. Upon arriving at the base, Erbeck was informed that he had orders to be deployed to Vietnam. He returned to Green Bay so he and Kathleen could be married quickly, then spent thirteen months overseas.

Bob VandeWalle happily collected his winnings from fellow Naval Academy cadets who put their money on the Cowboys.

Pam Duebler Oehldrich and her father, Chester, display their ticket stubs from the Ice Bowl. They celebrated every New Year's Eve together until Chester passed away in 2017. (Photo courtesy of Pam Duebler Oehldrich)

Brad Nuss, one of the fence jumpers at the Ice Bowl, spent much of his career as a human resources director for the State of Wisconsin. More than thirty years after the Ice Bowl, while serving as HR director at the Green Bay Correctional Institution, Nuss conducted orientation for new employees. A few weeks later, Nuss asked one of the new employees, Jim, how his work was going, and the conversation evolved into the Packers and football. Jim shared that he had actually snuck in to the Ice Bowl. Nuss said he did, too. They compared their stories and realized that Jim was one of the fourteen-year-old boys he had helped boost over the fence.

Cal Lawton returned to Chile many years later with his family, and it just happened to be at a time when the Packers were playing another playoff game. They ended up watching the game at the home of some Chileans.

Pam Duebler Oehldrich and her father, Chester, celebrated every New Year's Eve after the Ice Bowl by wearing their Ice Bowl shirts and sipping brandy in the presence of their goalpost souvenir. When Chester died in 2017, Pam buried the goalpost piece with him.

The Vanderloop brothers never expected to see their signed goalpost piece after it was sold from Whipp's Bar right after the Ice Bowl, although they kept the thin pieces they had cut off the end of it. Ed Vanderloop moved to Philadelphia, and more than

Ken (left) and Ed Vanderloop demonstrate how their thin slices of goalpost match up with a larger piece owned by a man Ed met in Philadelphia more than forty years later. (Photo courtesy Paul Vidani)

forty years after the Ice Bowl, attended a Packers game at Lincoln Financial Field. Seated near him was a man holding a goalpost piece with a chain connected to it to make sure he didn't lose it. In clear black letters on the goalpost piece were the names of Ken and Ed Vanderloop.

Ed Vanderloop approached the man, showed him his identification, and they agreed to rendezvous in Green Bay. Weeks later, the current owner of the goalposts met Ken and Ed Vanderloop at Austin Straubel Field for a picture. The brothers brought their short pieces of goal post to the meeting and were able to match them up with the longer piece.

David Bunker missed the game-winning play, but his father kept his ticket stub and later had it autographed by Jerry Kramer

This players bench from the Ice Bowl, relieved of its Lambeau Field duties after the game by Bob Murphy and Bob Kaminski, is on display in the Pro Football Hall of Fame. (Photo courtesy of Tom Murphy)

at the fiftieth anniversary of the Ice Bowl. Bunker also purchased a 50th Anniversary bottle of wine.

Frank Steffel's Ice Bowl story includes his taking some credit for the victory. He had worked in maintenance in the St. Vincent Hospital radiology department, and had been called in to help Kramer stand for X-rays that revealed the wood splinter in his spine. Steffel reasoned that if he hadn't helped stabilize Kramer that day, there wouldn't have been the goal-line block at the Ice Bowl.

The bench that Bob Murphy and Bob Kaminski pilfered sat for several years in Murphy's basement. Then he contacted the Pro Football Hall of Fame to see if there was interest in displaying it there. There was. The bench sits in the Packers section in Canton.

Murphy became ill with terminal cancer more than twenty years after the Ice Bowl. His son, Tom, visited Fuzzy Thurston's bar on Riverside Drive and met Jerry Kramer. When Thurston and Kramer heard the story of the bench, they drove to Murphy's house in Allouez and surprised him with a visit.

It was 2000 and members of the Ihlenfeldt family visited the Pro Football Hall of Fame in Canton, Ohio. Approaching the Packers' section of the Hall, they were met by an employee who told them about a great picture from the Ice Bowl that was on display there.

It was a picture of Fred Ihlenfeldt waving the bedsheet at the end of the game.

"This picture right here, that's my brother Fred, and that's me right there next to him at the Ice Bowl," Harlan Ihlenfeldt said. "We made that sign in our basement."

Bucky Ihlenfeldt (lower left) poses in front of a Pro Fooball Hall of Fame display featuring a photo of his uncle, Fred, holding a sign made from a bedsheet at the Ice Bowl. (Photo courtesy of Bucky Ihlenfeldt)

Jim Killinger, the dentist whose trip to the Ice Bowl was his first Packers experience, met a man at the game who became his dental partner, and that man's four daughters became the Killingers' babysitters for the next several years.

JoAnn Hanaway's legacy from the Ice Bowl was a lifelong sensitivity to cold weather. Her daughter, Maureen, who spent the Ice Bowl at home with a babysitter and a smashed thumb, became left handed.

Joe Bowers, who carried the players' bench out of Lambeau Field, eventually gave it to his brother-in-law and then lost track of it.

Sara Curtis, the widow of Michael Lefebvre, honored him every year on New Year's Eve. She and her sons would pose in front of the goalpost souvenir that they kept as a centerpiece on their dining room table. Sara then had a necklace made with a piece of the goalpost.

Sara Curtis holds a necklace she had made from a piece of the goalpost her late husband, Michael Lefebvre, was able to secure as a souvenir following the Ice Bowl. (Photo courtesy of Sara Curtis)

Mark Thompson, who was able to attend the Ice Bowl because of a thoughtful state trooper, eventually framed his ticket stub along with the towel that he lifted from the Packers sideline after the game. Years later, he and his wife, Barbara, operated an advertising and marketing business in Waukesha, and became corporate sponsors of the Packers Hall of Fame golf event and induction ceremony. It was at one of these events that Thompson was able to corner Packers running back Donny Anderson and talk about the Ice Bowl.

Mark Thompson created this display in his home from Ice Bowl and other Packers memorabilia. (Photo courtesy of Mark Thompson)

Thompson's paraphrase of Anderson's comment went: "Grabowski and I were the last of the 'bonus babies.' We were fortunate to have the money we got. I had an apartment with a heated garage. I get up, get dressed, get in the car, it starts. But as I'm driving to the stadium, I notice all these cars with their hoods up being jump-started. I figured I better get my breakfast taken care of and get on to the stadium. (In those days the players ate on their own.) I eat, get back in my car. It starts. I head to the stadium. Park. Get into the locker room. We're sitting around, smoking cigarettes and drinking bouilla ... Lombardi walks in and shouts 'Special Teams! Outside for warm-ups ... Anderson, stay here!' Apparently he didn't want me punting in the cold until I had to. So those of us still in the locker room knew how cold it was on the field when the special team guys came back in and Willie Wood's face was pale with frost from cheek-to-cheek!"

Paul Minten encountered friend Tom Vincent at their twentieth high school reunion and learned that Vincent was in an iconic picture showing him hanging from a goalpost at the Ice Bowl. His friend told him he helped carry the goalpost down Highland Avenue to a welder's shop, then went to a tavern on Broadway, but got kicked out and lost his goal posts. His brother, Joe, ended up with a trunk full of souvenir goalposts, tried to sell them in taverns, but no one wanted them, so threw them away in some farmer's field.

Tyler McCormack completed his tour in Vietnam eight months after the Ice Bowl. He returned to Wisconsin and became a middle school teacher in Wausau. But Gary Wayne Cooper, the Dallas soldier who stood guard duty with him listening to the Ice Bowl, was critically wounded a few months later, was returned to the United States, and died soon thereafter from his wounds. Years later, McCormack traveled to Washington, D.C., and located his fellow bridge guard's name on the Vietnam Memorial.

Joe Jarosh, who spent much of the Ice Bowl stomping his feet to keep them warm, didn't stray far from cold weather. His son, J.R., initiated the first Jacksonport Polar Bear Swim into Lake Michigan in 1986, and Joe spent the next twenty-five years as the event's emcee in Door County, Wisconsin.

Paul DeTennis displays the ladder that was to be used by the UW-La Crosse marching band at the Ice Bowl. The ladder resided for many years in the bar run by his father, Paul. (Photo courtesy of Paul DeTennis)

Gene Lamers was interviewed by Don Meredith's son, Michael, for his Ice Bowl documentary in 2017. Lamers still had the cape that had been on the quarterback's back during the Ice Bowl and kept it in his possession for the rest of his life. He relished the chance to repeat his story to anyone who would listen. When Lamers died in the summer of 2021, his son, Mike, brought the cape to the funeral and hung it on a coat rack at the back of the church.

The Cowboys cape that belonged to Bob Hayes didn't stay long at Paul's Bar in De Pere. Two weeks after the Ice Bowl, Packers trainer Bud Jorgenson and De Pere police officer Bob Ahasay came into the bar to retrieve the cape and send it back to Dallas. But the UW-La Crosse ladder found a home in the bar and remains on the property of the bar owner's son.

Thirty years after the Ice Bowl, *Fort Worth News-Telegram* sportswriter Frank Luksa reflected on what he called the most memorable game he ever covered.

"Other than memory of the Ice Bowl as c-c-c-old beyond description, I recall that it was impossible for Lambeau Field to freeze as solid as the Arctic polar cap. I had Vince Lombardi's assurance it could never happen.

"Lombardi's system worked fine on Saturday when the Cowboys went through a light romp. Relative to weather en route from Canada within 24 hours, it was springtime-calm and 12 degrees above zero. Heat from the coils collided with the cold air to create knee-high steam that rose into the air. It reminded me of an eerie scene on the moor in *The Hound of the Baskervilles*."

Luksa died in 2012.

Also in 1996, Bob St. John, who covered the Ice Bowl for the *Dallas Morning News*, recalled a humorous moment from Ice Bowl Day after he and Luksa had finished their locker room interviews.

"Frank and I were trudging across the tundra at Lambeau Field. We were carrying typewriters and luggage for a quick exit to the airport after we'd finished our stories.

"Suddenly, I heard a yelp, and Frank was gone. Just like that. Perhaps the Abominable Snowman had gotten him. But no. He'd slipped, sliding into a ditch, baggage and all, on his seat like a bobsled. I went for help, giving him my word if nobody showed up to help get him out, I'd return right after I finished my game story. Just kidding."

St. John died in 2017.

Leland Baenen, the dairy farmer who removed the goalpost padding before the fans removed the goalposts, sent a letter to Norm Schachter, who was the Ice Bowl referee, more than thirty years after the game.

Schachter wrote back: "I still get the shakes and shivers when I think of it. It was a great game. Every year about this time I get calls from different writers around the country."

In a 2000 interview, Schachter recalled how he was forced to call a timeout during the Packers' winning drive because a CBS network official notified him that it still had one more commercial to air. When Packers tackle Bob Skoronski asked him why he called the timeout, Schachter told him, "Players pension fund."

Schachter died in 2004.

Tony Shalhoub went on to a successful acting career, including the lead role in the TV series *Monk* and the voice of Luigi in the Pixar film *Cars*. One of the *Monk* episodes included a guest appearance by sportscaster Bob Costas, and the two men became friends.

Several years after the series ended, Costas went to Green Bay to broadcast a Packers game. While there, he called Tony Shalhoub and they got together for pizza where Tony and Dan Shalhoub were staying.

The subject of the Ice Bowl came up, and Costas started to tell a story about Cowboys defender George Andre, adding that Andre reportedly lost three toes as a result of the Ice Bowl and that he also had the misfortune of being blocked by Jerry Kramer on Starr's winning quarterback sneak.

Appleton native, Ice Bowl attendee, and former Pittsburgh Steelers running back Rocky Bleier (left) poses for a photo with Joe Bowers, who made his way onto the field and took photos during the Ice Bowl. (Photo courtesy of Joe Bowers)

Dan Shalhoub interrupted and said he thought the recipient of Kramer's block was actually Jethro Pugh. Costas leaped to his feet and said, "You're right. It was Jethro Pugh. I bow to your expertise."

Patti Kramer (Marholn) and her mother, Alice, reminded themselves every New Year's Eve of the special mother-daughter occasion that the Ice Bowl provided. But they also regretted that they hadn't kept any souvenirs from the game.

Then, the day of Alice's funeral in 2005, Patti and her daughter, Angela, were sorting through Alice's bedroom furniture when Angela came across something that didn't seem to fit in her grandmother's knitting drawer. It was the program from the Ice Bowl, in perfect condition. Alice must have forgotten that she stored it with her yarn and other supplies almost forty years earlier.

It was five years after the Ice Bowl and Rocky Bleier stood on the sidelines as a member of the Pittsburgh Steelers. The playoff game against the Oakland Raiders would come down to a final pass play since the Steelers trailed in the closing seconds.

Quarterback Terry Bradshaw went back to pass, but Bleier couldn't bear to watch. He turned his back. Later, he was able to watch the TV highlights of the deflected pass that Franco Harris caught and became known as the Immaculate Reception.

Two of the most iconic plays in NFL history and Bleier saw them both on TV replays.

Postscript

Pettis Norman, the Cowboys' tight end who played in the Ice Bowl, was in his sixth season with Dallas after signing as an undrafted free agent out of Johnson C. Smith University in 1962. He wrote his autobiography in 2021. In a communication to me, he granted permission to reprint these written comments about the impact of the Ice Bowl on him:

"I'll never forget the intensity of the hard hits and sub-zero cold, a field frozen as hard as concrete, the effects of the extreme conditions, the failure of the electric grid, hot chocolate and coffee freezing within minutes, and the emotions of the game. Some players had injuries to their mouths and noses that did not bleed due to sub-zero temperatures.

Pettis Norman, who played tight end for the Dallas Cowboys in the Ice Bowl, poses in his office alongside a commemorative Super Bowl football. (Photo courtesy of Pettis Norman)

"As we left Green Bay having lost, I reflected on the battle we had just endured. I reflected on Bart Starr's unbelievable last-seconds quarterback sneak. Several players had damaged lungs from the bitter cold and others almost lost their toes.

"All in all, the Ice Bowl is the most incredible game I ever played, an unbelievable experience that I've never forgotten. I look back and wonder how I got through it. I tell players now, 'Be thankful you don't have to play in those conditions.' "

***

John Niland was the Cowboys' starting left guard in the Ice Bowl, just two years out of the University of Iowa. He said he doesn't mind talking about the game as long as it isn't an intrusion.

"It was a good game," he said. "Unfortunately, we lost. It should never have been played. It was too cold. It was exhausting. It took me a long time to get back to the hotel."

Niland didn't want to talk to anybody after the game and decided not to get on the bus that took the team back to the hotel in Appleton. Instead, he hired a cab to drive him there.

"What can you do?" said Niland, 78, from his home in McKinley, Texas. "The game's over."

Former Dallas Cowboys guard John Niland (right) poses with fellow Cowboys alum Drew Pearson (left) and Texas business owner Randy Owens. (Photo courtesy of Shaughn Niland)

***

"There is no more iconic game in the history of the NFL than the Ice Bowl." - Brian Ditullio, *Bleacher Report*, 2010.

Acknowledgements

Recognition certainly goes to Paul (P.J.) Vidani of De Pere, whose network of Ice Bowl contacts proved to be both invaluable and extensive.

Sorting through the words and pictures, and making everything look and sound right, was the work of Mike Dauplaise of M&B Global Solutions Inc. in Green Bay.

But the majority of credit goes to those who kept the Ice Bowl memories and memorabilia alive and visible. They are the ones who refused to let the game die.

About the Author

Tony Walter has been telling stories of the Green Bay Packers and their fans for more than half a century, first as a writer and editor for the *Green Bay Press-Gazette*, and now in retirement through a series of three books.

His first effort, *Baptism by Football*, tells the story of the Packers' struggle to survive in their early years, focusing on the year 1922 and the cultural shift that was occurring in the post-World War I era. His second book, *The Packers, My Dad, and Me,* combines Tony's narration with that of his late father, John Walter. The book features entries from John Walter's personal diaries and his columns that appeared in the *Press-Gazette.*

Tony is a native of De Pere, Wisconsin, which is part of the Green Bay metropolitan area. After beginning his college education at Lawrence University in Appleton, Wisconsin, he completed his undergraduate studies at St. Norbert College in De Pere, the Packers' headquarters during summer training camp. Tony served in the United States Marine Corps Reserves from 1966-72.

In addition to his sports writing background, Tony covered the Wisconsin state government in Madison from 1973-76 and was a member of the prototype team for the new national newspaper USA TODAY in 1981. One of his career highlights was scoring a one-on-one interview in 2008 with then-Senator Barack Obama.

Tony received awards from the Wisconsin State School Boards Association, the Wisconsin Teachers Association, and won first place for sports writing from the National Sportswriters Association in 1983.

Tony has worked in youth ministry for the Episcopal Church for more than thirty-five years. He and his wife, Jenny, are the parents of two and grandparents of six.

Made in the USA
Columbia, SC
23 June 2022

62079728R00085